QUIZ TIME
MATHEMATICS

For Aspirants of Mathematical Olympiads,
NTSE and Students of All Age Groups

Published by:

F-2/16, Ansari Road, Daryaganj, New Delhi-110002
☎ 011-23240026, 011-23240027 • *Fax:* 011-23240028
Email: info@vspublishers.com • *Website:* www.vspublishers.com

Branch : Hyderabad
5-1-707/1, Brij Bhawan (Beside Central Bank of India Lane)
Bank Street, Koti, Hyderabad - 500 095
☎ 040-24737290
E-mail: vspublishershyd@gmail.com

Branch Office : Mumbai
Godown # 34 at The Model Co-Operative Housing, Society Ltd.,
"Sahakar Niwas", Ground Floor, Next to Sobo Central, Mumbai - 400 034
☎ 022-23510736
E-mail vspublishersmum@gmail.com

Follow us on:

All books available at **www.vspublishers.com**

© Copyright: V&S PUBLISHERS
ISBN 978-93-815886-8-0
Edition 2014

The Copyright of this book, as well as all matter contained herein (including illustrations) rests with the Publishers. No person shall copy the name of the book, its title design, matter and illustrations in any form and in any language, totally or partially or in any distorted form. Anybody doing so shall face legal action and will be responsible for damages.

Printed at : Param Offseters, Okhla, New Delhi-110020

Publisher's Note

In line with the range and series of Quiz Books published so far, V&S Publishers has come out with yet another novel and interesting *Quiz Time Mathematics* providing its readers with simple, interesting and brainteasing questions and quizzes along with their answers.

Since the year 2012 has been declared the 'National Mathematical Year' in India, this is definitely the ideal time to launch the book. The book is very concise and aims to develop and sharpen the logical, reasoning and mathematical skills of the readers, particularly the school and college going students.

The book is a unique blend of intriguing *Questions and Quizzes* divided into various chapters, such as *Numerals, Geometry and Algebra* defining the meaning of Mathematics, its various branches and usage, explaining the different, simple and complex mathematical terms and including the several theorems and laws to make the subject easier and interesting to the readers, especially the young students. Each chapter is accompanied with answers for the readers' convenience.

The book has also been made to cater to the needs of the students aspiring to qualify the Mathematical Olympiads, the National Talent Search Examination (NTSE), etc.

The Indian National Mathematical Olympiad (INMO) is an Olympiad in mathematics held in India. The INMO examination is conducted by the MO Cell in February of every year. School students of any class, starting from classes five and above first need to write the Regional Mathematical Olympiad of their respective state or region, usually held sometime between October and December of the previous year. Around 30 students are selected from each region, to write the INMO. Among these 400 or more students, a total of around 30 qualify the INMO.

The qualifying students are invited to a one month *mathematics camp* at the Homi Bhabha Centre for Science Education in Mumbai. In this camp, the students are taught Olympiad Mathematics and some other General Mathematics. *Five selection tests* are held during this period and the *top six students* in the selection tests qualify to represent India in the *International Mathematical Olympiad*.

So, go through the book thoroughly to sharpen your mathematical skills, qualify the above competitive tests if you are a keen aspirant as well as enjoy the thrill of solving these questions and quizzes.

Contents

1. **Branches of Mathematics** _____ 6
    Questions _____ 7
    Quizzes _____ 13
2. **Mathematical Words Origin** _____ 17
    Quizzes _____ 18
3. **Numerals** _____ 21
    Questions _____ 22
    Quizzes _____ 40
4. **Geometry** _____ 59
    Questions _____ 60
    Quizzes _____ 73
5. **Algebra** _____ 84
    Questions _____ 85
    Quizzes _____ 93

BRANCHES OF MATHEMATICS

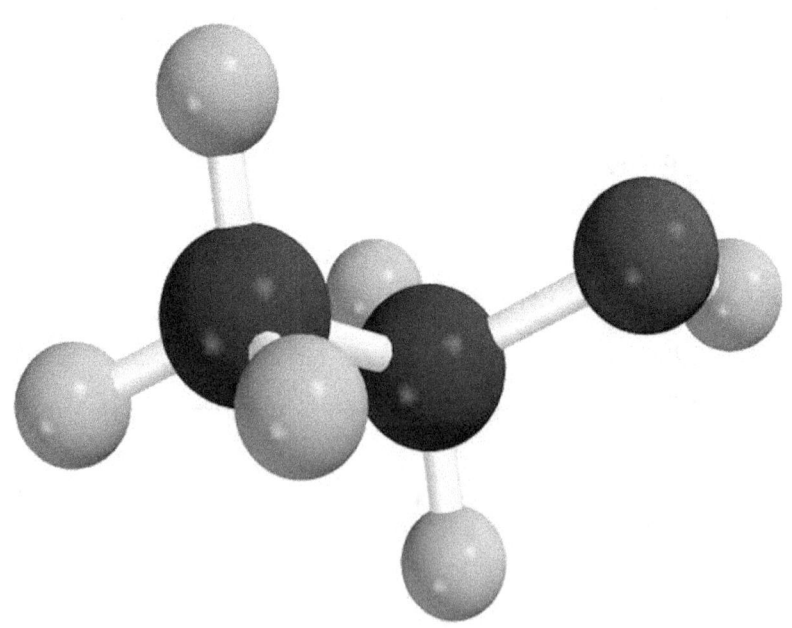

Branches of Mathematics

Questions

Q-1. What is mathematics?
Ans. The word 'mathematics' comes from the Greek word "mathematika", meaning "things that are learned". For ancient Greeks, mathematics included not only the study of numbers and space, but also astronomy and music. Nowadays, astronomy and music are not included in mathematics. In fact, it is the interdisciplinary tool of science.

Q-2. What are the two main branches of mathematics?
Ans. Mathematics is divided into two major branches: **Pure mathematics** and **Applied mathematics**. Pure mathematics is the study of quantities and their relationship, while applied mathematics is the use of pure mathematics to solve practical problems.

Q-3. What are the main branches of pure and applied mathematics?
Ans. The main branches of Pure Mathematics are Arithmetic, Algebra, Plane Geometry, Solid Geometry, Analytical Geometry, Non-Euclidean Geometry, Trigonometry, Calculus, etc. The main branches of Applied Mathematics are Statistics, Computers, Dynamics, Hydrostatics, Optics and Atomic Studies, etc.

Q-4. What is arithmetic?
Ans. Arithmetic is used to solve problems using numbers. It comes from a Greek word — "arithmos" meaning the science of numbers. It is the oldest and simplest branch of mathematics.

The fundamental operations of arithmetic are addition, subtraction, multiplication and division.

Q-5. What do we study in algebra?
Ans. Algebra deals with the whole group of numbers by means of symbols. Letters are used as symbols for numbers. Algebra uses equations and inequalities in solving problems. Sometimes algebra is also known as "Generalised Arithmetics."

Q-6. What is fluid dynamics?
Ans. It deals with the motion of bodies in liquids and gases.

Q-7. What is geometry?
Ans. It is a branch of mathematics, concerned with the properties of space, usually in terms of plane (two dimensional) and solid (three dimensional) figures.

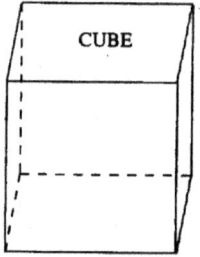
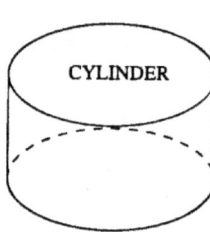

Q-8. What do we study in trigonometry?
Ans. Trigonometry is concerned with the triangle measurement. It makes use of the ratios of the sides of the triangle. It is of practical importance in navigating, surveying and simple harmonic motion in physics.

Q-9. What is analytical geometry?
Ans. It deals with generalised numbers and space relationship. In analytical geometry, we study planes and solid shapes with the help of coordinates. In analytical geometry, problems are solved using algebraic methods. It is also called coordinate geometry.

Branches of Mathematics

Q-10. What is calculus?
Ans. It deals with the study of different functions. It requires a knowledge of algebra, trigonometry and geometry. The two main branches of calculus are: Integral calculus and Differential calculus.

Q-11. Define integral calculus and differential calculus.
Ans. Integral calculus deals with the method of summation or adding together the effects of continuously varying quantities, while differential calculus deals in a similar way with rates of change.

Q-12. What do we study in biometry?
Ans. Biometry literally is the measurement of living things, but generally used to mean the application of mathematics to biology. The term is now largely obsolete, since mathematical and statistical works are the integral parts of most biological disciplines.

Q-13. What is demography?
Ans. The study related to population statistics is called demography.

Q-14. What is statistics?
Ans. Statistics is a branch of mathematics concerned with the manipulation of numerical information. It has two branches: descriptive statistics, dealing with the classification and presentation of data and analytical statistics, which studies the ways of collecting data, its analysis and interpretation. Sampling is the fundamental to statistics.

Q-15. What is statics?
Ans. Statics is an applied branch of mathematics which deals with the mathematics and physics of the bodies at rest. It deals with the forces acting on structures.

Q-16. What is dynamics?
Ans. Dynamics is the mathematical and physical study of the behaviour of bodies under the action of forces that produce changes of motion in them.

Quiz Time Mathematics

Q-17. What is hydrostatics?
Ans. It deals with the properties and behaviour of liquids, specially the forces in liquids at rest.

Q-18. What is aerodynamics?
Ans. It deals with the motions of body in air. It is closely related with aeronautics because it studies the flight of aeroplanes and other machines that are heavier than air.

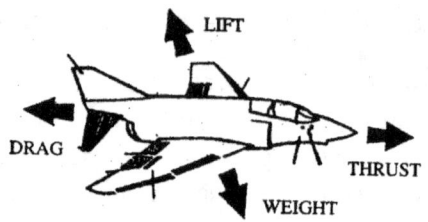

Q-19. What is hydrodynamics?
Ans. It deals with the motion of bodies in liquids. 'Hydro' stands for water and 'dynamics' for motion.

Q-20. What is dimensional analysis?
Ans. Dimensional analysis deals with the dimensions of physical quantities, such as mass (M), length (L) and time (T) and the derived units are obtainable by multiplication or division from such quantities.

Q-21. With which branch of mathematics the system analysis is associated?
Ans. The system analysis is associated with computer science.

Q-22. What is econometrics?
Ans. The application of mathematics and statistics to solve the problems of economics is called econometrics.

Q-23. How do we define logic and theory of games?
Ans. The logic and the theory of games are two fields of mathematics concerned with the study of decision making. Logic

Branches of Mathematics

and game theory are closely related and, in some circumstances, a combination of both may be required.

Q-24. What is topology?
Ans. Topology is a branch of geometry concerned with general transformation of shapes in which certain correspondence points is preserved. Topology mainly deals with surfaces.

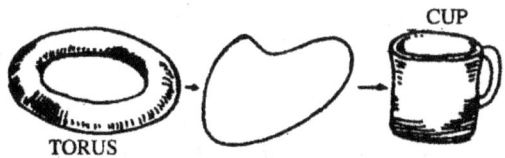

Q-25. What is numerical analysis?
Ans. Numerical analysis is the general study of methods for solving complicated problems using basic operations of arithmetic. Development of digital computers has made numerical analysis a very important area of applied mathematics.

Q-26. What is Linear programming?
Ans. Linear programming is a mathematical modelling technique useful for guiding quantitative decisions in business planning, industrial engineering and in the social and physical sciences. It is of recent origin but has become an important part of applied mathematics.

Q-27. What is operational research?
Ans. It is a branch of mathematics which makes use of scientific methods to the management and administration of organised military, governmental, commercial and industrial systems.

Q-28. What is number theory?
Ans. It is the branch of mathematics concerned with the abstract study of the structure of number systems and the properties of positive integers of natural numbers, such as 1, 2, 3, 4, etc.

Q-29. What is mathematical theory of optimisation?
Ans. Mathematical theory of optimisation is a technique of improving or increasing the value of some numerical quantity that in practice may take the form of temperature, air flow, speed, pay off in a game, information, monetary profit and the like.,

Q-30. How do we define Probability?
Ans. The branch of mathematics which expresses chance in number statements is called probability. For example, if a person tosses a coin, there are two ways it can fall, *head* or *tail*. So probability or chance of getting a tail or head in a toss of a coin is one half.

Q-31. Which branch of science belongs to both physics and mathematics?
Ans. Computer science belongs to both physics and mathematics. This deals with the structure and operation of computer systems, their underlying design and programming principles and techniques for the practical implementation of computer hardware and software in various areas.

Q-32. Which branch of mathematics deals with informations?
Ans. Information theory. It is the branch of mathematics which deals with the transmission and processing of information. It was developed by an American engineer, Cloude E. Shannon in 1948. It has been found very useful in automation of communication systems.

Q-33. What is matrix in mathematics?
Ans. Matrix in mathematics, is a square or rectangular array of elements. They are a means of condensing information about mathematical systems and can be used for among other things, solving of simultaneous linear equations.

Branches of Mathematics

Quizzes

1. Game Theory, a branch of mathematics is attributed to −
   - Ⓐ. David Hilbert
   - Ⓑ John Von Newmen
   - Ⓒ Kurt Godel
   - Ⓓ Euler

2. The bridges of Koinsberg game birth to a new branch of mathematics called −
   - Ⓐ Topology
   - Ⓑ Game Theory
   - Ⓒ Probability Theory
   - Ⓓ Game Theory

3. Antonine Parent had presented his first work on analytical geometry of ____ dimensions.
   - Ⓐ 2
   - Ⓑ 3
   - Ⓒ 4
   - Ⓓ 5

4. The idea of polar co-ordinate is due to −
   - Ⓐ Descartes
   - Ⓑ Leibnitz
   - Ⓒ Gregorio Fontana
   - Ⓓ De Moivre

5. Who is called the creator of vector analysis?
   - Ⓐ Gauss
   - Ⓑ Hermann Grassmarm
   - Ⓒ Peacock
   - Ⓓ Pythagoras

6. Which branch of mathematics had its origin from painting?
   - Ⓐ Graph Theory
   - Ⓑ Operational Research
   - Ⓒ Projective Geometry
   - Ⓓ Informative Theory

Quiz Time Mathematics

7. The bridge of Koingsberg had helped to originate one branch of mathematics called –
   - Ⓐ Topology
   - Ⓑ Linear Programming
   - Ⓒ Tensor Analysis
   - Ⓓ Boolean Algebra

8. Modern analytical geometry is called Cartesian geometry on the name of –
   - Ⓐ Euclid
   - Ⓑ Thales
   - Ⓒ Descartes
   - Ⓓ Diophantus

9. The Theory of Relativity given by Einstein is based on –
   - Ⓐ Euclidean Geometry
   - Ⓑ Riemannian Geometry
   - Ⓒ Projective Geometry
   - Ⓓ Graph Theory

10. Who coined the new branch Functional Analysis in mathematics?
    - Ⓐ Abel
    - Ⓑ Banach
    - Ⓒ Dedekind
    - Ⓓ Bayes

11. The Euclidean geometry is based on five postulates; the first four are point, straight line, circle and right angle. What is the fifth postulate?
    - Ⓐ Parallel postulate
    - Ⓑ Congruence
    - Ⓒ Plane
    - Ⓓ Similar

12. The study of geometry and trigonometry of figures on the surface of a sphere is called –
    - Ⓐ Projective geometry
    - Ⓑ Acturial Science
    - Ⓒ Spherics
    - Ⓓ 3-D-Geometry

13. An Applied branch of mathematics which deals with the mathematics and physics of the bodies at rest is called?
    - Ⓐ Dynamics
    - Ⓑ Calculas
    - Ⓒ Statics
    - Ⓓ Projective Geometry

Branches of Mathematics

14. Which branch of mathematics is the system analysis associated?
    - Ⓐ Dynamics
    - Ⓑ Calculas
    - Ⓒ Statics
    - Ⓓ Computer Science

15. Which branch of mathematics deals with the transmission and processing of information?
    - Ⓐ Topology
    - Ⓑ Information Theory
    - Ⓒ Infosys
    - Ⓓ Trigonometry

16. Which branch of mathematics deals with the application of mathematics and statistics to solve the problems of economics?
    - Ⓐ Economical Mathematics
    - Ⓑ Information Technology
    - Ⓒ Econometrics
    - Ⓓ Dimensional Analysis

Quiz Time Mathematics

Answers

1.	A	7.	A	13.	C
2.	A	8.	C	14.	D
3.	B	9.	B	15.	B
4.	C	10.	B	16.	C
5.	B	11.	A		
6.	C	12.	C		

MATHEMATICAL WORDS ORIGIN

Quiz Time Mathematics

Quizzes

1. The word 'fraction' is derived from a Latin word called –
   - Ⓐ Fractus
   - Ⓑ Fracions
   - Ⓒ Frangere
   - Ⓓ Friend

2. Who coined the term Co-ordinate, Ordinate and Abscissa used in Analytical Geometry?
   - Ⓐ Archimedes
   - Ⓑ Descartes
   - Ⓒ Leibnitz
   - Ⓓ Diophantus

3. Who used the term commutative and distributive in the usual algebraic sense in mathematics?
   - Ⓐ Hamilton
   - Ⓑ Newton
   - Ⓒ Servois
   - Ⓓ Napier

4. Who suggested the term Linear Programming to Dantzig?
   - Ⓐ I J Koopmans
   - Ⓑ Stigner
   - Ⓒ Laderman
   - Ⓓ Hooper

5. Who coined the term Mathematical Induction to mathematics?
   - Ⓐ Leibniz
   - Ⓑ De Morgan
   - Ⓒ L' Hospital
   - Ⓓ Apollonous

6. Who coined the term Matrix in mathematics?
   - Ⓐ Gauss
   - Ⓑ Euler
   - Ⓒ Sylvester
   - Ⓓ Fleming

Mathematical Words Origin

7. Who had coined the term focus in Conic Section?
   - Ⓐ Apollonius
   - Ⓑ Kepler
   - Ⓒ Lagrange
   - Ⓓ L'Hospital

8. Who used the word sin to indicate the ratio of perpendicular to hypotenuse in trigonometry?
   - Ⓐ Diophantus
   - Ⓑ Edmund Gunter
   - Ⓒ Brahmagupta
   - Ⓓ Wallis

9. Who suggested the use of simplex method in the LPP (Linear Programming Problem)?
   - Ⓐ Cayley
   - Ⓑ Weirestrass
   - Ⓒ Dantzig
   - Ⓓ Sylvester

10. Pythagoras had coined the term Mathematics. What was the meaning given by Pythagoras for Mathematics?
    - Ⓐ That which is learned
    - Ⓑ Interesting
    - Ⓒ Calculation
    - Ⓓ That which helps in business

11. The word Algebra is derived from the title of a work written by Al-Khowarizmi al-jabr-wal-muqabalah. For what does the word al-Jabr stand?
    - Ⓐ Deaf
    - Ⓑ dump
    - Ⓒ Reunion of broken parts
    - Ⓓ calculation

12. Arithmetic is derived from the word Arithmetika, what does it mean?
    - Ⓐ The number theory
    - Ⓑ Calculation
    - Ⓒ The number science
    - Ⓓ Digging earth

13. Percentage has the origin from the Latin word_____
    - Ⓐ Percentum
    - Ⓑ percentium
    - Ⓒ Percenti
    - Ⓓ Permutation

Quiz Time Mathematics

Answers

1.	C	6.	C	11.	C
2.	B	7.	B	12.	C
3.	C	8.	B	13.	A
4.	A	9.	C		
5.	B	10.	A		

NUMERALS

Quiz Time Mathematics

Questions

Q-1. How did our ancestors count the things?
Ans. The people first used pebbles or knots or marks of ten fingers of hands for counting the number of animals in a herd.

Q-2. When did people use symbols to represent numbers?
Ans. The man created symbols to represent numbers as soon as he learned to write.

Q-3. What is the meaning of word, numeral?
Ans. The symbol that is used to write a number is called numeral.

Q-4. How did our ancestors keep count of their sheep?
Ans. Every morning as they let the sheep out, they made marks on a tree — one mark for each sheep. In the evening, when they brought the sheep back, they matched each sheep with the mark on the tree. In this way, they could tell if there was any change in the number of sheep.

Numerals

Q-5. What familiar things were used for counting by the ancient man?

Ans. Several familiar things were used for counting by the ancient man. Lion's head was used to indicate one, wings of an eagle to indicate two, leaves of a clover to indicate three and so on.

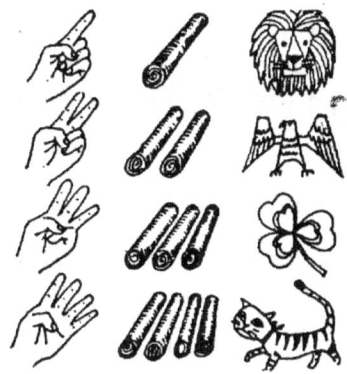

Q-6. How did the Babylonians represent numbers?

Ans. The Babylonians used to write numbers on flat bricks of wet clay with sharp-edged sticks. Their number representations from 1 to 10, 100, 1000 are shown in the figure below.

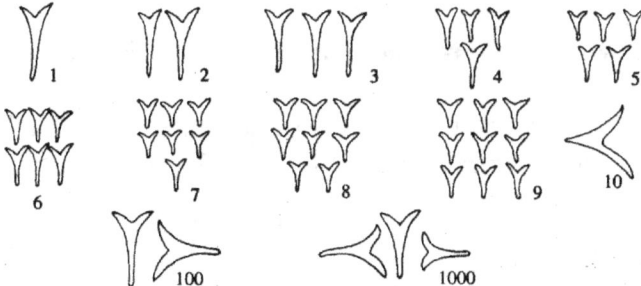

Q-7. When did the Babylonians develop cuneiform numerals?

Ans. The Babylonians developed the cuneiform or wedge-shaped writing for numbers, some 5000 years ago.

Quiz Time Mathematics

Q-8. How can we write 243 in Babylonian numerals?
Ans. We write symbol of 100 twice, symbol of 10 four times and then the symbol of 3.

Q-9. What was the system of numerals developed by the ancient Egyptians?
Ans. Hieroglyphic system. They used this system for decorative purpose on stone monuments.

Q-10. How were the numbers represented in the hieroglyphic system?
Ans.

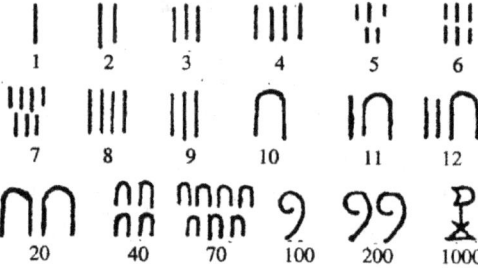

Q-11. Was there any symbol for zero in the ancient Chinese system?
Ans. No, there was no symbol for zero, and a gap had to be left to indicate it. For example, the number, 7004 was written as

⊥ |||

Q-12. What was the other numeral system of the ancient Egyptians?
Ans. Another number system used by the ancient Egyptians was called the hieratic number system. It was more efficient

Numerals

than the hieroglyphic system. It served them in their day-to-day computations.

Q-13. How did the Greeks write numbers?
Ans. The Greeks used all the letters of their alphabet plus three additional symbols for writing numbers. The first nine symbols represented the numbers from one to nine; the next nine, the tens from ten to ninety; the last nine, the hundreds from one hundred to nine hundred. They had no symbol for zero. To represent thousands, the Greeks added a bar to the left of the first nine letters.

$$
\begin{array}{cccccccccccccc}
A & B & \Gamma & \Delta & E & F^* & Z & H & \Theta & I & K & \Lambda & M & N \\
1 & 2 & 3 & 4 & 5 & 6 & 7 & 8 & 9 & 10 & 20 & 30 & 40 & 50
\end{array}
$$

$$
\begin{array}{cccccccccc}
\Xi & O & \Pi & Q^* & P & \Sigma & T & \Upsilon & \Phi & X & \Psi & \Omega & \overline{b}^* \\
60 & 70 & 80 & 90 & 100 & 200 & 300 & 400 & 500 & 600 & 700 & 800 & 900
\end{array}
$$

Q-14. What was the method used by Hebrews for writing numbers?
Ans. The Hebrews also used their alphabet for writing numbers.

נ מ ל כ י ט ח ז ו ה ד ג ב א
1 2 3 4 5 6 7 8 9 10 20 30 40 50

ם ץ ן ף ץ צ פ ק ר ש ת ד ס ו ע
60 70 80 90 100 200 300 400 500 600 700 800 900

Q-15. What was the system for writing numbers used by the ancient Chinese? How did the Chinese write numbers more than ninety?
Ans. The ancient Chinese used rod like symbols to represent numbers. The hundreds were written in the same way as the units. For example, the symbol, II would stand for either two or two hundred depending upon its position in the number. Thousands were written in the same way as tens, the ten

thousand in the same way as the units and so on. The number 7684 was written as

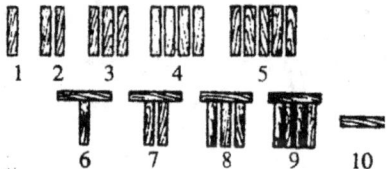

Q-16. How did the ancient Japanese write numbers?

Ans. The ancient Japanese used short wooden sticks to represent numbers as shown in the figure below.

Q-17. During the thirteenth and fourteenth century, what was the form of receipt in former USSR for taxes collected by officers?

Ans. The form of receipts of the taxes was as shown in the figure below. This receipt shows an amount of 3674 rubles and 46 kopecks (1 ruble equals to 100 kopecks).

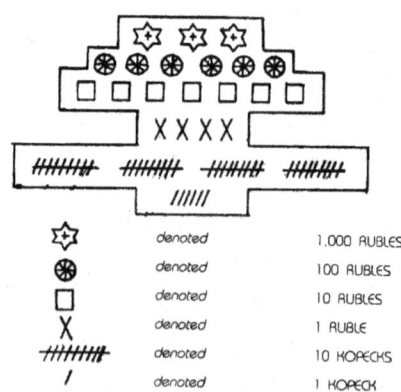

Numerals

Q-18. What is the Roman system of numerals?

Ans. The Roman system of numbers was probably derived from Etruscans, the earlier inhabitants of Italy. Letters were used for numerals. I stood for one, V stood for five, X for ten, L for fifty, C for a hundred, D for five hundred and M for a thousand.

I	II	III	IV	V	VI	VII	VIII	IX
1	2	3	4	5	6	7	8	9

X	XX	L	C	D	M	CMC
10	20	50	100	500	1000	10000

Q-19. How do we write different numbers in the Roman system of numerals?

Ans. In the Roman system, two is represented as II, three as III. An I is put before V to write four. If the symbol of a smaller number preceeded the symbol of a larger number, the smaller number is to be subtracted from the larger (subtractive principle). For example, the symbol for nine is IX. The symbol for six is VI, for seven is VII, for eight is VIII. From these, we see that if a number is smaller than the number that follows it, it is subtracted from the second number; if it is larger than the following number, the second number is added to it. Thus, LX stands for sixty but XL stands for forty.

Q-20. Where did the Hindu-Arabic system of numerals originate?

Ans. The Hindu-Arabic system of numerals originated in India and was later adopted by the Arabs. The Hindu-Arabic numerals of the tenth century are shown in the figure below.

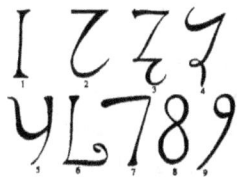

Quiz Time Mathematics

Q-21. Which was the system of numbers used by the Mayans of Central America?
Ans. Their system of numbers also included zero.

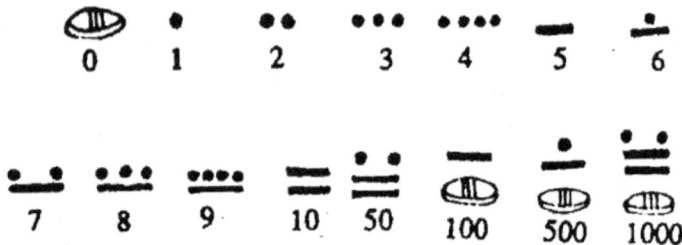

Q-22. Where was zero invented?
Ans. The idea of zero was originally invented in India. It was introduced to Europe and took the form we know it today. As a matter of fact, zero was used in 628 A.D. by well-known Indian mathematician Brahmagupta for carrying out six operations of mathematics. The word, 'zero' evolved from the Sanskrit word, *shunya* meaning, nothing. It became *sifer* in Arabic from which the English word, 'cipher' is derived. Leonardo Fibonacci latinised it to 'zephirum', and finally, a Florentine treatise, *'De Arithmetica Opusculum'* established the word, zero once for all in 1491.

Q-23. What are the unique properties of zero?
Ans. The unique properties of zero are:
   a) When zero is placed to the right of 1, the number becomes ten. By continuing to put zeros to the right of 1, we make the value of 1 ten times greater for every zero.
   b) If zero is put to the left of 1 with a decimal point before it, the value becomes one-tenth. Two zeros, make it one-hundredth and so on.

Numerals

c) Any number, except zero, multiplied by zero, the result is always zero.

d) Any number, except zero, divided by zero, the result is undefined.

e) Addition or subtraction of zero does not alter the result.

f) Zero divided by any number, except zero, the result is always zero.

Q-24. How did the Spanish write numbers around 1000 AD?
Ans. See the given figure.

Q-25. What is the modern system of numerals?
Ans. It is the modified Hindu-Arabic system in which we write numbers from one to nine and zero as 1,2,3,4,5,6,7,8,9, and 0. The base of our system is ten and so, it is called a decimal system (decem means ten in Latin). It is a place value system in which the position of a symbol indicates its particular value. Any number, no matter how large, can be written with the help of these ten digits.

Q-26. How did the Italians write numerals around 1400 AD?
Ans.

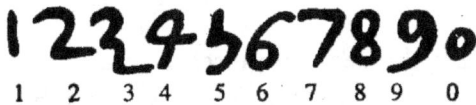

Quiz Time Mathematics

Hindu-Arabic and Roman equivalents						
Hindu-Arabic	Roman	How we pronounce	Hindu-Arabic	Roman	How we pronounce
0	nil	nought, nothing, zero	17	XVII	seventeen
1	I	one	18	XVIII	eighteen
2	II	two	19	XIX	nineteen
3	III	three	20	XX	twenty
4	IV	four	21	XXI	twenty-one
5	V	five	30	XXX	thirty
6	VI	six	40	XL	forty
7	VII	seven	50	L	fifty
8	VIII	eight	60	LX	sixty
9	IX	nine	70	LXX	seventy
10	X	ten	80	LXXX	eighty
11	XI	eleven	90	XC	ninety
12	XII	twelve (a dozen)	100	C	one hundred
13	XIII	thirteen	101	CI	one hundred and one
14	XIV	fourteen	144	CXLIV	one gross
15	XV	fifteen	288	CCLXXXVIII	two gross
16	XVI	sixteen	1000	M	one thousand

Q-27. Which numeral system is in common use today?

Ans. The Hindu-Arabic numerals are in common use today. These numerals are 0, 1, 2, 3, 4, 5, 6, 7, 8 and 9. This is a decimal system.

1	2	3	4	5
6	7	8	9	0

Q-28. What is the decimal presentation?

Ans. The decimal presentation is done by a dot. For example, 0.3 is read as zero point three. The dot is called decimal point. 0.3 is

Numerals

equal to 3/10. Similarly, 0.01 is 1/100 and 0.001 is 1/1000 and so on. The place next to decimal point is the tenths position, the one next to it is the hundredths position and so on. The numbers such as 2.3 are called mixed decimals. The numbers which have one number before the decimal point and some after it are called mixed decimals.

Q-29. What are the even natural numbers?
Ans. Any number which is exactly divisible by 2 is called an even number. For example, 2, 4, 6, 8, etc., are the even natural numbers.

Q-30. What are the odd natural numbers?
Ans. The numbers which are not divisible by 2 are called the odd numbers, such as 1, 3, 5, 7, 9, ... etc.

Q-31. What is meant by the infinite set of numbers?
Ans. The series of numbers 1,2,3, ... is infinite. That is, it has no end.

Q-32. What is a fraction, and how is it represented?
Ans. Fraction in mathematics is a number that indicates one or more equal parts of a whole. The numerator of a fraction is written above the dividing line and the denominator below the dividing line. For example, 3/8 is a fraction. 3 is the numerator and 8 is the denominator. It shows that a whole number is divided into 8 parts of which 3 are taken.

Q-33. What are proper and improper fractions?
Ans. When the numerator is less than the denominator, the fraction is called proper fraction. An improper fraction has a numerator that is larger than the denominator, for example, 3/2.

Q-34. What is a decimal fraction?
Ans. Decimal fraction has as its denominator a power of 10, and these are omitted by use of decimal point and notation, for example, 0.04 which is 4/100.

Q-35. What are factors?
Ans. The factors of a number are all the numbers which will divide it exactly without leaving a remainder. For example, 18 has six factors: 1, 2, 3, 6 and 18.

Q-36. What is the rule of division of powers?
Ans. The numbers written in their index forms can be divided by subtracting 8 to their indices. For example, $5^8 + 5^3 = 55$.

Q-37. If a number is raised to some power and then the whole is raised to some other power, what would be the result?
Ans. If a number say, 7 is raised to the power 2, we write 7^2. If 7^2 is raised to the power 3 then we write $(7^2)^3$. The result would be 7^6, i.e., when a power is raised by some other power, the indices get multiplied.

Q-38. What are perfect numbers?
Ans. The perfect number is a whole number which equals the sum of all its factors other than the number itself. Perfect numbers are rare. For example, 6 and 28 are perfect numbers.

Q-39. What are powers or indices?
Ans. When a number is multiplied by itself, it is said to have been raised to the power of two. For example, $5 \times 5 = 5^2$, $5 \times 5 \times 5 = 5^3$. The number written above is called the power or index, and the number written below is called the base.

Q-40. What are negative powers?
Ans. A negative power or index shows how many times one must be divided by the number. For example, $7^{-1} = 1/7$, $7^{-5} = 1/7^5$.

Q-41. What is the rule of multiplication of powers?
Ans. The numbers written in their index forms can be multiplied by adding their powers. For example, $5^2 \times 5^6 = 5^8$

Numerals

Q-42. What is the meaning of the root of a number?
Ans. If a large number can be written as the power of a smaller number, the smaller number is called a root of the large number. For example, $32 = 2^5$, 2 is, therefore, the fifth root of 32 and can be written as or $32^{1/5}$.

Q-43. What is a complimentary number?
Ans. In the number theory, the number which is obtained by subtracting a number from its base is called a complimentary number. For example, the compliment of 7 in numbers to the base, 10 is 7.

Q-44. What are rational numbers?
Ans. Rational numbers are those numbers that can be expressed as the ratio of two integers. They include all positive and negative integers as well as any number that can be expressed as a fraction.

Q-45. What is a square root and a cube root?
Ans. If a number is raised to the power 1/2, it is called the square root of the number. Similarly, if a number is raised to the power 1/3, it is called cube root of the number. For example, square root of 64 is 8, while cube root is 4. The sign of root is ($\sqrt{}$).

Q-46. What are prime numbers?
Ans. A prime number is any positive integer (excluding 1) having no integral factors other than itself and unity. It is a natural number which cannot be expressed as the product of other natural numbers. For example, 2, 3, 5, 7, 11, 13, etc. are prime numbers. The lowest prime number is thus 2. The highest known prime number is 2216091 discovered in September 1985. This prime number contains 65050 digits. The lowest non-prime (excluding 1) number is 4.

Q-47. What are irrational numbers?
Ans. The numbers which are not rational are called irrational numbers. They cannot be expressed as the ratio of two integers.

Q-48. How would you judge whether a number is divisible by 2?
Ans. A number is divisible by 2, if its last digit is divisible by 2, i.e., its last digit is even.

Q-49. What is the criterion that a number is divisible by 3?
Ans. A number is divisible by 3, if the sum of its digits is divisible by 3. For example, 531 is divisible by 3 because the sum of its digits, (5+3+1=9) is divisible by 3.

Q-50. How would you ascertain that a number is divisible by 4?
Ans. If the number formed by the last two digits of a number is divisible by 4, the original number is divisible by 4. For example, 732 is divisible by 4 because its last two digits form 32, which is divisible by 4.

Q-51. What is the criterion that a number is divisible by 5?
Ans. If the last digit of a number is 0 or 5, it is divisible by 5.

Q-52. How can we decide that a number is divisible by 6?
Ans. If a number is divisible by both 2 and 3, it is divisible by 6.

Q-53. How would you test that a number is divisible by 7?
Ans. To check the divisibility by 7, start at the right and separate the digits into groups of three. Beginning with +, write + and − alternately in front of each group. Do the sum and if the answer is a multiple of 7, then the original number is divisible by 7. For example, 14294863492 is divisible by 7 because -- 14+294 - 863+492= - 91=7×-13.

Q-54. What is the criterion of divisibility by 8?
Ans. If the number formed by the last three digits of a number is divisible by 8, the number is divisible by 8.

Q-55. What is the criterion that a number is divisible by 9?
Ans. If the sum of the digits of the number is a multiple of 9, the number is divisible by 9.

Numerals

Q-56. How would you check that a number is divisible by 10?
Ans. A number is exactly divisible by 10, if its last digit is 0.

Q-57. What are triangular numbers?
Ans. If the dots representing a number can be arranged into a triangle, it is called the triangular number. See the figure below.

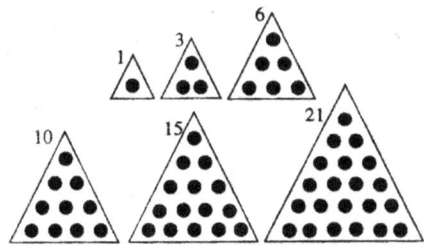

Q-58. What are polygonal numbers?
Ans. When a number is represented by a group of dots such that the dots, can be arranged in a geometric shape, it is called a polygonal number.

Q-59. What are square numbers?
Ans. If the dots representing a number can be arranged into a square, the number is called a square number (Figure)

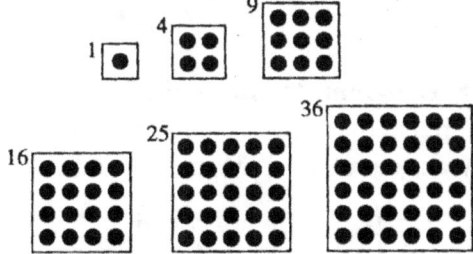

Q-60. What are cubic numbers?
Ans. The numbers which can be represented by three dimensional cubes.

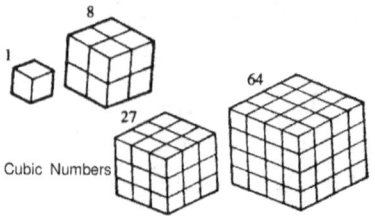
Cubic Numbers

Q-61. What is lowest common multiple?
Ans. The smallest number among the common multiples of two numbers is called their Lowest Common Multiple (LCM). For example, LCM of 4 and 6 is 12.

Q-62. What are the laws of multiplication?
Ans. There are three laws of multiplication:
      (i) The Commutative Law
      (ii) The Associative Law
      (iii) The Distributive Law

Q-63. What are tetrahedral numbers?
Ans. The numbers that can be represented by the layers of triangles forming a tetrahedron are called tetrahedral numbers.

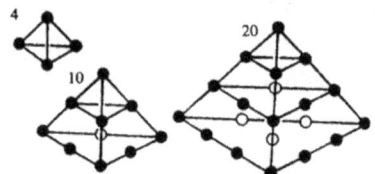

Q-64. What are pyramidal numbers?
Ans. The numbers that can be represented as layers of squares forming a pyramid are called pyramidal numbers.

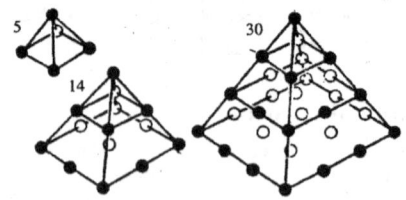

Numerals

Q-65. What are the basic operations of numbers?
Ans. Addition, subtraction, multiplication and division are the four basic operations of numbers.

Q-66. What is addition?
Ans. Calculating the total of two or more numbers is called addition. By adding one number to another, we get their sum.

Q-67. What are the laws of addition?
Ans. There are two laws of addition:
  (i) Commutative law of addition
  (ii) Associative law of addition

Q-68. What is the commutative law of addition?
Ans. The sum of two numbers does not change even if the order of addition is changed.

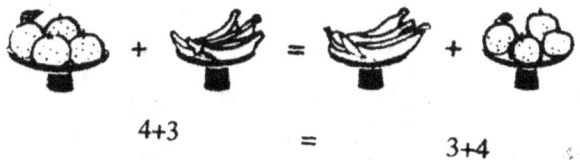

4+3 = 3+4

Q-69. What is the associative law of addition?
Ans. For three numbers, (A+B)+C=A+(B+C). This is called the associative law.

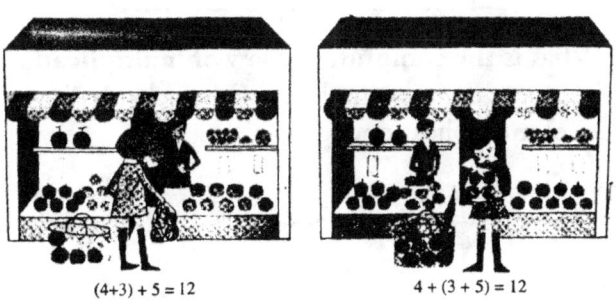

(4+3) + 5 = 12   4 + (3 + 5) = 12

Quiz Time Mathematics

Q-70. What is a common multiple?
Ans. A number which is a multiple of two different numbers at the same time is called their common multiple. For example, 2 is a common multiple of 4 and 6. Similarly, 5 is a common multiple of 15 and 20.

Q-71. What is subtraction?
Ans. The difference of the two numbers is called subtraction.

Q-72. What is multiplication?
Ans. Multiplication is the process of repeated addition as many times as a number is being multiplied by another number. It is a way of combining two numbers to obtain a third number, symbolised by 'Y'. For example, 4×5=20, it means 4 is repeatedly added 5 times.

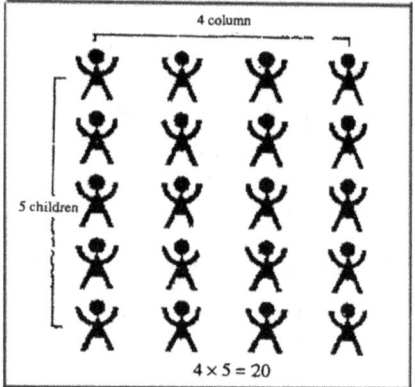

Q-73. What is the commutative law of multiplication?
Ans. The product of two numbers does not change, if we change the order of multiplication.

Numerals

Q-74. What is the associative law of multiplication?
Ans. The multiplication (A×B)×C is the same as A×(B×C). This is called the associative law of multiplication.

Q-75. What is the distributive law of multiplication?
Ans. According to this law, the value of A×(B+C) = A×B+A×C.

Q-76. What is division?
Ans. The process of repeated subtraction is called division. On doing repeated subtraction, we may or may not get some remainder.

Q-77. Explain the terms divisor, dividend, quotient and remainder?
Ans. See the example below:

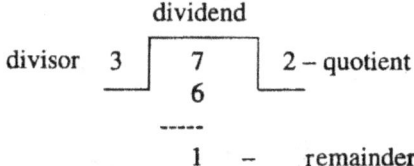

Q-78. What is a common factor?
Ans. When a number is a factor of two numbers, this is called the common factor of the two numbers. For example, 3 is a factor of 6, and 3 is also a factor of 9. So, 3 is a common factor of 6 and 9.

Q-79. What is the highest common factor?
Ans. The product of the set of common factors of two numbers is called the Highest Common Factor (HCF). For example, common factors of 12 and 18 are 2 and 3. Their product is 6, so their highest common factor is 6.

Q-80. What are the positive numbers?
Ans. The numbers which are greater than zero are called positive numbers.

Quiz Time Mathematics

Quizzes

1. How many digits are there in the Hindu-Arabic system?
   - Ⓐ 10
   - Ⓑ 20
   - Ⓒ 30
   - Ⓓ 40
2. In Roman Numerals, M represents 1000, what does $\overline{M}$ represent?
   - Ⓐ 10000
   - Ⓑ 50000
   - Ⓒ 100000
   - Ⓓ 500
3. What does D represent in the Roman numerals system?
   - Ⓐ 100
   - Ⓑ 1000
   - Ⓒ 5000
   - Ⓓ 500
4. If 5=V, How is 5000 written in the Roman numerical system?
   - Ⓐ $\overline{V}$
   - Ⓑ MMMMM
   - Ⓒ MX
   - Ⓓ MV
5. What is the smallest Natural number?
   - Ⓐ 1
   - Ⓑ 0
   - Ⓒ −1
   - Ⓓ 10100
6. What is the smallest Whole number?
   - Ⓐ 1
   - Ⓑ 0
   - Ⓒ −1
   - Ⓓ 10^{100}
7. Among the following, which natural number has no predecessor?
   - Ⓐ 100
   - Ⓑ 1
   - Ⓒ 1729
   - Ⓓ googal

Numerals

8. Which among the following is the largest known number in the world?
   - Ⓐ ∞
   - Ⓑ googal
   - Ⓒ googalplex
   - Ⓓ crore

9. What does 1 googal mean?
   - Ⓐ 1 followed by hundred zeros
   - Ⓑ 1 followed by thousand zeros
   - Ⓒ 1 followed by ten thousand zeros
   - Ⓓ 1 followed by 1 lac zeros

10. How is one googalplex represented?
    - Ⓐ 1 googalplex = 100googal
    - Ⓑ 1 googalplex = 10googal
    - Ⓒ 1 googalplex = 10 lac
    - Ⓓ 1 googalplex = ∞

11. Among the following, which whole number has no predecessor?
    - Ⓐ -1
    - Ⓑ 0
    - Ⓒ 1
    - Ⓓ e

12. Counting numbers are kept under:
    - Ⓐ Natural Number
    - Ⓑ Whole Number
    - Ⓒ Rational Number
    - Ⓓ Real Number

13. An integer that is divisible by 2 is called:
    - Ⓐ Even Number
    - Ⓑ Natural Number
    - Ⓒ Odd Number
    - Ⓓ Whole Number

14. A set of numbers which include 0 and the counting number is called:
    - Ⓐ Even Number
    - Ⓑ Natural Number
    - Ⓒ Odd Number
    - Ⓓ Whole Number

15. The whole number is denoted by –
    - Ⓐ N
    - Ⓑ R
    - Ⓒ W
    - Ⓓ Q

Quiz Time Mathematics

16. **All counting numbers, together with their negatives and zero constitutes the set of:**
    - Ⓐ Whole Number
    - Ⓑ Real Number
    - Ⓒ Integers
    - Ⓓ Odd Number

17. **The number in the form of $\frac{p}{q}$, where p and q are integers and q ≠ 0 is called:**
    - Ⓐ Rational Number
    - Ⓑ Irrational Number
    - Ⓒ Real Number
    - Ⓓ Hexagonal Number

18. **$\sqrt{2}, \sqrt{3}, \sqrt{5}...$ are the examples of which of the following set of number?**
    - Ⓐ Rational Number
    - Ⓑ Irrational Number
    - Ⓒ Real Number
    - Ⓓ Complex Number

19. **A number which is expressed as a +ib, where a and b are reals, are called:**
    - Ⓐ Rational Number
    - Ⓑ Complex Number
    - Ⓒ Real Number
    - Ⓓ Irrational Number

20. **An integer p which is not 0 or + 1 and is divisible by no integer, except + 1 and itself is called:**
    - Ⓐ Rational Number
    - Ⓑ Pefect Number
    - Ⓒ Prime Number
    - Ⓓ Complex Number

21. **Who said:**

    "Upon looking at prime numbers, one has the feeling of being in presence of one of the inexplicable phenomena one site of creation."
    - Ⓐ Pythogoras
    - Ⓑ Hipparcus
    - Ⓒ Donzager
    - Ⓓ Eratosthenes

22. **Where was the idea of zero invented?**
    - Ⓐ America
    - Ⓑ Europe
    - Ⓒ India
    - Ⓓ Italy

Numerals

23. **Who said:**
    "The importance of the creation of the zero mark can never be exaggerated. This which gives us airy nothing not merely a local habitation, a name, a picture, a symbol, but helped power is characteristics of the Hindu race from which it sprang. It is like coining the NIRVANA into the dynamos. No single mathematical creation has been ever patent for the general on go of intelligence and power."
    - Ⓐ Einstein
    - Ⓑ G B Halsted
    - Ⓒ Aryabhatta
    - Ⓓ Newton

24. **The method to find the primes between two numbers was given by:**
    - Ⓐ Einstein
    - Ⓑ Euler
    - Ⓒ Eratosthenes
    - Ⓓ Wilson

25. **"Every even number except 2 is the sum of two prime numbers." This statement is better known as:**
    - Ⓐ Goldback Conjecture
    - Ⓑ Wilson Theorem
    - Ⓒ De Polignac Theorem
    - Ⓓ Berland Theorem

26. **There is always at least one prime number between n and 2n-2 provided n is greater than 3. Who stated this conjecture?**
    - Ⓐ Goldbach
    - Ⓑ Bertand
    - Ⓒ Wilson
    - Ⓓ Eratosthenes

27. **There are only primes between 9,999,900 to 10,000,000.**
    - Ⓐ 9
    - Ⓑ 10
    - Ⓒ 100
    - Ⓓ 121

28. **p, p+2, p+4, are called...... if all numbers are primes.**
    - Ⓐ Pythagorean triplet
    - Ⓑ Prime triplet
    - Ⓒ Lucas number
    - Ⓓ Fermat triplet

29. There are only 2 primes between 10,000,000 to 10,000,100. One is 10,000,019. What is the other prime?
    - Ⓐ 10,000,037
    - Ⓑ 10,000,067
    - Ⓒ 10,000,079
    - Ⓓ 10,000,097

30. 1, 4, 9, 16, 25, 36.... are the examples of
    - Ⓐ Square Number
    - Ⓑ Pythagorean Number
    - Ⓒ Lucas Number
    - Ⓓ Ramanujan Number

31. 1, 8, 27, 64, 125.... are the examples of
    - Ⓐ Triangular Number
    - Ⓑ Lucas Number
    - Ⓒ Cubic Number
    - Ⓓ Square Number

32. 1, 3, 6, 10.... are the example of
    - Ⓐ Triangular Number
    - Ⓑ Lucas Number
    - Ⓒ Cubic Number
    - Ⓓ Square Number

33. 4, 10, 20, 35, 56 ... are the examples of
    - Ⓐ Tetrahedral Number
    - Ⓑ Square Number
    - Ⓒ Pyramid Number
    - Ⓓ Lucas Number

34. If the sum of cubes of each digits of a number is equal to the number itself, the number is called:
    - Ⓐ Kaprekar Number
    - Ⓑ Lucas Number
    - Ⓒ Armstrong Number
    - Ⓓ Square Number

35. A number is called....... number if it is equal to the sum of all of its factors, except itself.
    - Ⓐ Kaprekar Number
    - Ⓑ Defective Number
    - Ⓒ Perfect Number
    - Ⓓ Cardinal Number

36. A special number $Ø = \frac{\sqrt{5}+1}{2}$ is known as:
    - Ⓐ Golden Number
    - Ⓑ Pythagoras Number
    - Ⓒ Ordinal Number
    - Ⓓ Cardinal Number

Numerals

37. Two numbers are called .... number if each of which is equal to the sum of all the exact divisors of the other, except the number itself.
    - Ⓐ Palindromic Number
    - Ⓑ Amicable Number
    - Ⓒ Armstrong Number
    - Ⓓ Abundant Number

38. A number 'n' is called abundant if the sum of all of its divisors is more than:
    - Ⓐ 2n
    - Ⓑ 2n
    - Ⓒ n2
    - Ⓓ 22n

39. Which among the following is the first abundant number?
    - Ⓐ 12
    - Ⓑ 220
    - Ⓒ 1729
    - Ⓓ 945

40. The smallest odd abundant number is:
    - Ⓐ 1945
    - Ⓑ 5000
    - Ⓒ 1937
    - Ⓓ 945

41. p and e are:
    - Ⓐ Happy Numbers
    - Ⓑ Sad Numbers
    - Ⓒ Transcendental Numbers
    - Ⓓ Algebraic Numbers

42. 6, 15, 28, 45... are the examples of
    - Ⓐ Hexagonal Numbers
    - Ⓑ Tetranedral Numbers
    - Ⓒ Pyramid Numbers
    - Ⓓ Euler Numbers

43. 635318657 is the smallest number which can be expressed as the sum of two fourth power in two different ways.
    $6335318657 = 133^4 + 134^4$
    $= 59^4 + 158^4$

    What is this special number called?
    - Ⓐ Harshad Number
    - Ⓑ Happy Number
    - Ⓒ Euler Number
    - Ⓓ Fermat Number

44. Number of the type $F^n = 2^{2^n} + 1$ is called:
    - (A) Fermat Number
    - (B) Kaprekar Number
    - (C) Fibonacci Number
    - (D) Happy Number

45. Numbers which remain the same when read from left to right or vice-versa, e.g 15151, 121, etc. are called:
    - (A) Defective Numbers
    - (B) Pythagoras Numbers
    - (C) Palindromic Numbers
    - (D) Fibonacci Numbers

46. Which among the following is the largest even prime number?
    - (A) 2
    - (B) 3
    - (C) 8
    - (D) 0

47. What is the smallest odd prime number?
    - (A) 2
    - (B) 3
    - (C) 9
    - (D) 11

48. What does LCD stand for –
    - (A) Low Cost Depot
    - (B) Lower Coded Decimal
    - (C) Least Common Denominator
    - (D) Liberal Criminal Department

49. Which among the following is known as Beast number or Devil's number?
    - (A) 945
    - (B) 6174
    - (C) 666
    - (D) 2157

50. Bhaskaracharya in his famous book, "Bijganita" writes: "In the quantity consisting of that which has zero for its divisor, there is no alteration, though many may be inserted or extracted; as no change takes place in the infinite and immutable God when worlds are created or destroyed, though numbers and orders of beings are absorbed or put forth."

Numerals

About which mathematical symbol this quotation is talking about?
- Ⓐ Zero
- Ⓑ Pie
- Ⓒ Infinity
- Ⓓ Addition

51. $1+\frac{1}{11_0}+\frac{1}{21_0}+\frac{1}{31_0}$ is represented by a mathematical symbol. What is it?
- Ⓐ π
- Ⓑ e
- Ⓒ Ø
- Ⓓ ∞

52. Which number is shown by the prefix "Uni"
- Ⓐ 0
- Ⓑ 1
- Ⓒ 10
- Ⓓ 2

53. 1 mile = ... km.
- Ⓐ 10
- Ⓑ 1.254
- Ⓒ 1.6093
- Ⓓ 330

54. 1 inch = ... centimetre.
- Ⓐ 2.54
- Ⓑ 0.99
- Ⓒ 1.6093
- Ⓓ 643

55. What does LCDLIX in Roman numeral stand for?
- Ⓐ 61745
- Ⓑ 5387
- Ⓒ 50549
- Ⓓ 43281

56. How many times in a day are the hands of a clock straight?
- Ⓐ 12
- Ⓑ 22
- Ⓒ 24
- Ⓓ 44

57. How many times are the hands of a clock at 90° in a day?
- Ⓐ 24
- Ⓑ 36
- Ⓒ 44
- Ⓓ 12

58. How many times do the hands of a clock coincide in a day?
    - (A) 24
    - (B) 22
    - (C) 20
    - (D) 21

59. How many times do the hands of a clock point towards each other in a day?
    - (A) 24
    - (B) 20
    - (C) 22
    - (D) 21

60. The number of prime factors in $2^{222} \times 3^{333} \times 5^{555}$ is:
    - (A) 1110
    - (B) 1107
    - (C) 329
    - (D) 3

61. Out of 2^{2^2}, 2^{22}, 222, $(22)^2$, which one is the largest?
    - (A) 2^{2^2}
    - (B) 2^{22}
    - (C) 222
    - (D) $(22)^2$

62. If A is irrational, B is irrational, then their product AB is:
    - (A) Irrational
    - (B) Rational
    - (C) Transcedental
    - (D) Perfect

63. The process of converting a binary number system into its decimal equivalent is known as:
    - (A) Double-Bubble
    - (B) Hexagonal
    - (C) Nim game
    - (D) Hubble-Bubble

64. The symbol that is used to write a number is called –
    - (A) Rational
    - (B) Numeral
    - (C) Numeric
    - (D) Mathematics

65. What was the system of numerals developed by the ancient Egyptians?
    - (A) Hieroglyphic
    - (B) Cuneiform
    - (C) Chinese
    - (D) Japanese

Numerals

66. The modern system of numerals is known as decimal system. What does the Latin word, Decem mean?
    - Ⓐ Ten
    - Ⓑ Twenty
    - Ⓒ Zero
    - Ⓓ Two

67. Any number which is not divisible by 2 and expressible in the form of 2n+1 is called?
    - Ⓐ Even Number
    - Ⓑ Odd Number
    - Ⓒ Whole Number
    - Ⓓ Integers

68. A Rational number is represented by:
    - Ⓐ N
    - Ⓑ Z
    - Ⓒ Q
    - Ⓓ R

69. Integers are represented by:
    - Ⓐ N
    - Ⓑ Z
    - Ⓒ Q
    - Ⓓ R

70. Which number has exactly one factor?
    - Ⓐ 10
    - Ⓑ 1
    - Ⓒ 2
    - Ⓓ 3

71. How many factors does a prime number have?
    - Ⓐ 2
    - Ⓑ 8
    - Ⓒ 7
    - Ⓓ 3

72. In a + 0 = a, Here 0 is called:
    - Ⓐ Additive Identity
    - Ⓑ Multiplicative Inverse
    - Ⓒ Whole Number
    - Ⓓ Prime Number

73. In a × 1= a, is known as:
    - Ⓐ Additive Identity
    - Ⓑ Multiplicative Identity
    - Ⓒ Additive Inverse
    - Ⓓ Multiplicative Inverse

Quiz Time Mathematics

74. Which among the following is the smallest 3-digit perfect square?
    - (A) 100
    - (B) 961
    - (C) 225
    - (D) 724

75. Which among the following is the greatest 3-digit greatest square?
    - (A) 100
    - (B) 961
    - (C) 141
    - (D) 396

76. Which among the following is the smallest 4-digit perfect square?
    - (A) 1225
    - (B) 1024
    - (C) 9801
    - (D) 3225

77. Which among the following is the greatest 4-digit perfect square?
    - (A) 1225
    - (B) 1024
    - (C) 9801
    - (D) 7225

78. Any two consecutive primes which differ by 2 are known as:
    - (A) Prime Doublet
    - (B) Twin Primes
    - (C) Mersenne Primes
    - (D) Co-prime

79. Square number cannot end with 2, 3, 7 and –
    - (A) 8
    - (B) 5
    - (C) 6
    - (D) 9

80. How many numbers are there between 1 and 100 that are both square and cubic?
    - (A) 8
    - (B) 5
    - (C) 4
    - (D) 2

81. How many symbols do we use in a binary code number?
    - (A) 2
    - (B) 3
    - (C) 8
    - (D) 16

Numerals

82. 1, 3, 4, 7, 11…….. is the example of –
    Ⓐ Fibonacci Number
    Ⓑ Lucas Number
    Ⓒ Fermat Number
    Ⓓ Even Number

83. 1, 1, 2, 3, 5, 8, 13, 21... is the example of –
    Ⓐ Fibonacci Number
    Ⓑ Fermat Number
    Ⓒ Square Number
    Ⓓ Lucas Number

84. Which among the following is the smallest perfect number?
    Ⓐ 28   Ⓑ 424
    Ⓒ 6   Ⓓ 3

85. The largest cube in the Fibonacci sequence is:
    Ⓐ 27   Ⓑ 64
    Ⓒ 1331   Ⓓ 9

86. What is the least number that can be expressed as the sum of cubes of the first two numbers?
    Ⓐ 8   Ⓑ 9
    Ⓒ 1729   Ⓓ 6174

87. What is the sum of the square of the first two odd numbers?
    Ⓐ 10   Ⓑ 20
    Ⓒ 30   Ⓓ 40

88. In which numeral system, there is no symbol for zero –
    Ⓐ Hindi-Arabic system
    Ⓑ Greeks
    Ⓒ Roman Numeral system
    Ⓓ International system

89. In Oxford museum, there is a royal mace on which there is a record of 120000 prisoners, 400000 captive oxen and of 1422000 captive goats. In which numerals, these numbers are written?
   - Ⓐ Hieroglyphs
   - Ⓑ Roman
   - Ⓒ Arabic
   - Ⓓ Hindu

90. $\sqrt{2}, \sqrt{3}, \sqrt{5}, \ldots$ are the examples of Surds. Which is originated from the Latin word "Surdus". What is its meaning?
   - Ⓐ Deaf
   - Ⓑ Dumb
   - Ⓒ Lame
   - Ⓓ Blind

91. What is the sum of the first 100 natural numbers?
   - Ⓐ 5000
   - Ⓑ 5050
   - Ⓒ 10000
   - Ⓓ 100

92. What is the sum of the first 10 odd numbers?
   - Ⓐ 100
   - Ⓑ 200
   - Ⓒ 300
   - Ⓓ 400

93. What is the sum of the first 20 even numbers?
   - Ⓐ 400
   - Ⓑ 420
   - Ⓒ 395
   - Ⓓ 470

94. 1729, 4104, 13832, ... are the examples of –
   - Ⓐ Ramanujan-Hardy Number
   - Ⓑ Hardy Number
   - Ⓒ Harshad Number
   - Ⓓ Euler Number

95. $\frac{1}{2}, \frac{1}{4}, \frac{1}{8}, \frac{1}{16}, \frac{1}{32}$.... such fractions having 1 as the numerator was called .... by the Egyptians.
   - Ⓐ Horus Eye Fraction
   - Ⓑ Horus Hand Fraction
   - Ⓒ Horus Leg Fraction
   - Ⓓ Horus Ear Fraction

96. Which of the following is the amicable number pair?
   - Ⓐ (220, 284)
   - Ⓑ (120, 130)
   - Ⓒ (290, 340)
   - Ⓓ (135, 154)

Numerals

97. Which of the following are Happy numbers?
    - Ⓐ 19
    - Ⓑ 28
    - Ⓒ 35
    - Ⓓ 65

98. A number that is divisible by the sum of its digits is called:
    - Ⓐ Ramanujan Number
    - Ⓑ Harshad Number
    - Ⓒ Archimedes Number
    - Ⓓ Platonic Number

99. The fear of 13 is called:
    - Ⓐ Triskaidekaphobia
    - Ⓑ Claustrophobia
    - Ⓒ Xenobhobia
    - Ⓓ Hydrophobia

100. Among the following, which number is called the Euler number?
    - Ⓐ 1729
    - Ⓑ 635318657
    - Ⓒ 1741725
    - Ⓓ 656565444

101. (3, 4, 5), (5, 12, 13) (6, 8, 10), (7, 24, 25)... are called-
    - Ⓐ Triangular Numbers
    - Ⓑ Pythagorean Triplet
    - Ⓒ Octagonal Numbers
    - Ⓓ Pentagonal Numbers

102. A number of the form 2" that contains the digit, 666 is called:
    - Ⓐ Fibonacci Number
    - Ⓑ Apocalyptic Number
    - Ⓒ Amicable Number
    - Ⓓ Avogadro Number

103. It is believed that the Egyptians used a specific number id for their construction of pyramids. What was the number?
    - Ⓐ Golden Number
    - Ⓑ Fibonacci Number
    - Ⓒ Triangular Number
    - Ⓓ Archimedes Number

104. Which civilisation used the sexagesmial system in mathematics?
    - Ⓐ Egyptian
    - Ⓑ Babylonian
    - Ⓒ Indus
    - Ⓓ Italian

Quiz Time Mathematics

105. 1729 is called
    - (A) Harshad Number
    - (B) Euler Number
    - (C) Ramanujan Number
    - (D) Happy Number

106. .... is called the Kaprekar Number.
    - (A) 1729
    - (B) 6174
    - (C) 8128
    - (D) 25658

107. Who discovered the Irrational Number?
    - (A) Pythogoras
    - (B) Plato
    - (C) Pappus
    - (D) Aristotle

108. In Vigesimal system, the base is taken as:
    - (A) 2
    - (B) 3
    - (C) 20
    - (D) 4

109. In which number system, the odd number always ends in 1 and the even number always ends in 0?
    - (A) Binary
    - (B) Octagonal
    - (C) Hexagonal
    - (D) Pyramid

110. Which book of Plato deals with the Mystic number?
    - (A) Theaetetus
    - (B) Platonicus
    - (C) Republic
    - (D) Principia

111. What is the use of ARLC test?
    - (A) It is a technique to test prime number.
    - (B) It is a technique to test the divisibility.
    - (C) It is a technique to test the square root of a number.
    - (D) It is a technique to find the cube root of a number.

112. Which number is equal to the cube of the sum of its digits?
    - (A) 1729
    - (B) 15625
    - (C) 4913
    - (D) 1728

Numerals

113. Which number follows the property ab× cd = abcd?
    - Ⓐ 2592
    - Ⓑ 1374
    - Ⓒ 1729
    - Ⓓ 6174

114. Who proved that ϖ2 is irrational?
    - Ⓐ Lambert
    - Ⓑ Legendre
    - Ⓒ Shanks
    - Ⓓ Aryabhata

115. Greek Philosopher Plato had fixed the population for a model town, what was the number?
    - Ⓐ 5040
    - Ⓑ 10000
    - Ⓒ 6174
    - Ⓓ 1729

116. Which two digit numbers is equal to the area and perimeter of a square?
    - Ⓐ 16
    - Ⓑ 25
    - Ⓒ 36
    - Ⓓ 64

117. A number which is obtained by subtracting a number from its bases is called?
    - Ⓐ Rational Number
    - Ⓑ Complimentary Number
    - Ⓒ Square Number
    - Ⓓ Social Number

118. A number system which has its base, 8 is called?
    - Ⓐ Octal Number
    - Ⓑ Hexagonal Number
    - Ⓒ Quibinary
    - Ⓓ Octagon Number

119. $2^{-1}, 2^{-2}, 2^{-3}, \ldots$ are called
    - Ⓐ Binary Numbers
    - Ⓑ Binomial Numbers
    - Ⓒ Bicimal
    - Ⓓ Hindu Arabic Numbers

120. What does BCD stand for?
    - Ⓐ Bharat Criminal Department
    - Ⓑ Bureau of Criminal Defence
    - Ⓒ Binary Coded Decimal
    - Ⓓ Binary Code for Division

121. The famous division, lemma, a = bq + r, where q and r are respectively quotient and remainder, was given by a famous mathematician. Who was he?
- Ⓐ Euclid
- Ⓑ Pythagoras
- Ⓒ Pappus
- Ⓓ Euler

122. The greatest number in Rigveda is –
- Ⓐ 10^{12}
- Ⓑ 10^6
- Ⓒ 60099
- Ⓓ 74532

123. The highest number mentioned in Yajurveda is
- Ⓐ 10^{12}
- Ⓑ 10^{100}
- Ⓒ 10^{18}
- Ⓓ 10^7

124. In which system, the alphabet
A=10   B=11   C=12
D=13   E= 14   F= 15
is represented?
- Ⓐ Hex System
- Ⓑ Binary System
- Ⓒ Tertiary System
- Ⓓ Bicimal

Numerals

Answers

#	Ans	#	Ans	#	Ans
1.	A	19.	B	39.	A
2.	C	20.	C	40.	D
3.	D	21.	C	41.	C
4.	A	22.	C	42.	A
5.	A	23.	B	43.	C
6.	B	24.	C	44.	A
7.	B	25.	A	45.	C
8.	C	26.	B	46.	A
9.	A	27.	A	47.	B
10.	B	28.	B	48.	C
11.	B	29.	C	49.	C
12.	A	30.	A	50.	C
13.	A	31.	C	51.	B
14.	D	32.	A	52.	B
15.	C	33.	A	53.	C
16.	C	34.	C	54.	A
17.	A	35.	C	55.	C
18.	B	36.	A	56.	D
		37.	B	57.	C
		38.	A	58.	B
				59.	C
				60.	D
				61.	B
				62.	A

Quiz Time Mathematics

63.	A	84.	C	105.	A, C
64.	B	85.	D	106.	B
65.	A	86.	B	107.	A
66.	A	87.	A	108.	C
67.	B	88.	C	109.	A
68.	C	89.	A	110.	C
69.	B	90.	A	111.	A
70.	B	91.	B	112.	C
71.	A	92.	A	113.	A
72.	A	93.	B	114.	A
73.	B	94.	A	115.	A
74.	A	95.	A	116.	A
75.	B	96.	A	117.	B
76.	B	97.	A	118.	A
77.	C	98.	B	119.	C
78.	B	99.	A	120.	C
79.	A	100.	A	121.	A
80.	D	101.	B	122.	C
81.	A	102.	B	123.	A
82.	B	103.	A	124.	A
83.	A	104.	A		

GEOMETRY

Quiz Time Mathematics

Questions

Q-1. What is Plane Geometry?
Ans. Plane Geometry is the branch of mathematics which deals with points, lines, angles, triangles, quadrilaterals, circles, etc. The word 'geometry' has originated from the Greek word, 'geometric' which means earth measurement.

Q-2. Who was Thales?
Ans. Thales (640 – 546 B.C.) was a Greek mathematician and scientist. He made advances in geometry and predicted sun's eclipse in 585 B.C. He discovered that no matter what diameter one draws in a circle, it always cuts the circle into two halves.

Q-3. Who is called the Father of Geometry?
Ans. The learned Greek mathematician, Euclid, who taught Geometry at the Museum of Alexandria in Egypt about 300 B.C. His major work the Elements is still the basis of much of Geometry.

Q-4. What is a theorem?
Ans. A theorem is a statement that gives certain facts about a figure and one concludes from these facts that certain other facts must be true. Advanced mathematics consists almost entirely of theorems and proofs, but even at a simple level theorems are very important.

Q-5. What was the contribution of Euclid to geometry?
Ans. Euclid systematised the total knowledge of geometry and presented it in 13 volumes called *Elements*. These volumes

Geometry

contain information about points, lines, circles, triangles, methods of making geometrical figures, theories of ratio and proportion and various theorems of geometry. The last three volumes deal with solid geometry.

The solid and plane geometries are together called Euclidean geometry which is based on self-evident postulates.

His main work lay in the systematic arrangements of previous discoveries and the geometrical book remained a standard textbook for over 2000 years, and are still in regular use today.

Q-6. What is a postulate in geometry?
Ans. In geometry, one cannot prove certain statements of relations between figures. Such statements are called postulates. One example of a postulate is, "only one straight line can be drawn between two points."

Q-7. How do we define a point in geometry?
Ans. A point is the simplest element in geometry. It has neither length nor width or thickness. A geometric point is impossible to make because it has no dimensions.

Q-8. What is a line?
Ans. A collection of points is called a line and the shortest distance between the two points is called a straight line. The line has only length. It does not have any width or thickness.

Q-9. What is a ray?
Ans. The name ray, is given to the part of a line that starts at a given point.

Q-10. What are parallel lines?
Ans. The lines which meet at infinity are called parallel lines (Fig.). Railway tracks are parallel lines.

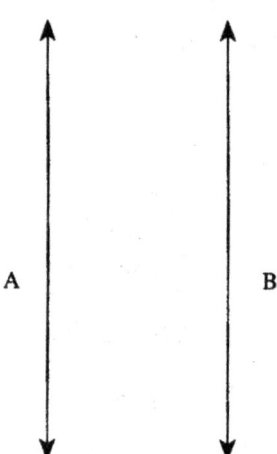

Q-11. What is a plane?
Ans. A plane is a surface having two dimensions. For example, the surface of a table top is a plane.

Q-12. How are angles named according to their sizes?
Ans. Angles are named as follows:

- (a) Acute angle – It measures more than 0°, but less than 90°.
- (b) Right angle – It measures 90°.
- (c) Obtuse angle – It measures more than 90°, but less than 180°.
- (d) Straight angle – It measures 180°.
- (e) Reflex angle – It measures more than 180°, but less than 360°.

Geometry

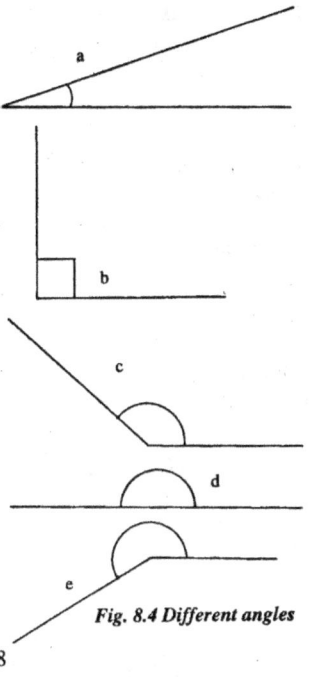

Fig. 8.4 Different angles

Q-13. What is an angle?

Ans. An angle in mathematics, is the amount of turn or rotation; it may be defined by a pair of rays (half-line) that share a common end point, but do not lie in the same line. AB & BC are two rays with the same standing point. The angle formed by these two rays is, ∠ABC.

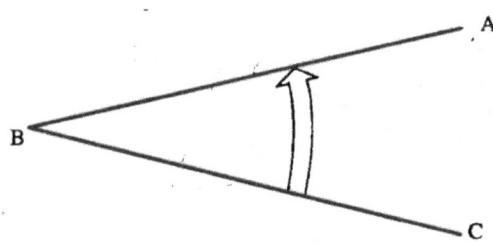

Q-14. What are the complementary angles?

Ans. The complementary angles are two angles whose sum is 90°.

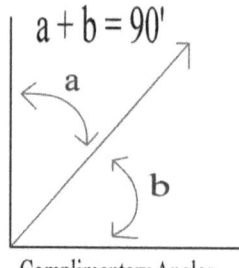

Complimentary Angles

Q-15. What are the equal triangles?

Ans. The triangles having the same size or area are called the equal triangles.

Q-16. What are the supplementary angles?

Ans. The supplementary angles are two angles whose sum is 180°.

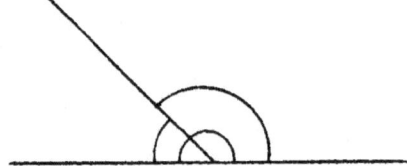

Q-17. What are the conjugate angles?

Ans. The conjugate angles are two angles whose sum is 360°.

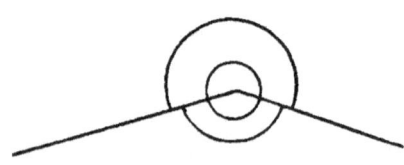

Geometry

Q-18. What is a triangle?
Ans. A plane figure bounded by three line segments is called a triangle. The sum of the internal angles of a triangle is always 180°.

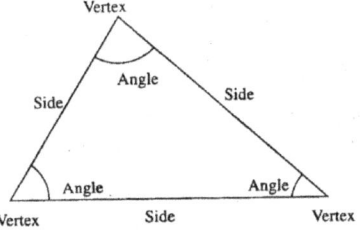

Q-19. How are triangles classified?
Ans. Triangles are classified as:
  (a) Acute angled triangle: A triangle with three acute angles. (i.e. less than 90').
  (b) Right angled triangle: A triangle that contains one right angle. The hypotenuse is the side opposite the right angle.
  (c) Obtuse angled triangle: A triangle that contains one obtuse angle. (i.e., more than 90°)

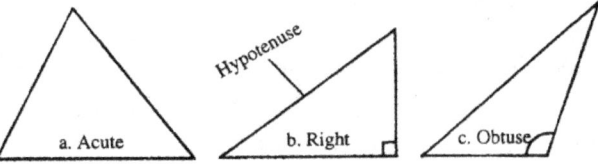

Q-20. What is an equilateral triangle?
Ans. In an equilateral triangle, all the sides are of the same length and all the angles are equal to 60°.

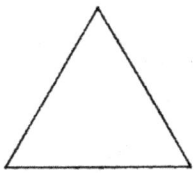

Q-21. What is an ellipse?

Ans. An ellipse is a curve, joining all the points around two fixed points so that the sum of the distances from those points is always constant. Those two points are called foci of the ellipse.

Q-22. What is an isosceles triangle?

Ans. A triangle whose two sides are equal and two angles are the same or equal.

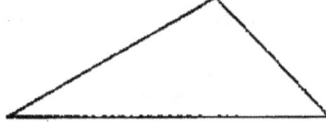

Q-23. What is a scalene triangle?

Ans. A triangle whose all sides and angles are of different sizes.

Q-24. Which is the most famous theorem of triangles?

Ans. In geometry, the most famous theorem is the Pythagoras theorem which states that in a right-angled triangle, the square of the hypotenuse (the longest side) is equal to the sum of the squares of lengths of the other two sides.

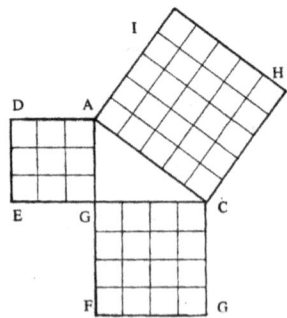

Geometry

Q-25. What are similar triangles?
Ans. The triangles having the same shape, but different sizes are called similar triangles.

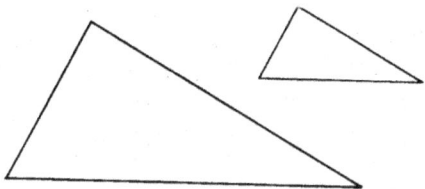

Q-26. What is a median?
Ans. A line which joins the midpoint of one side of a triangle to the opposite vertex is called median.

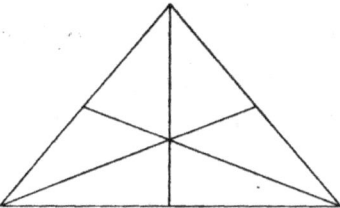

Q-27. What is a quadrilateral?
Ans. A quadrilateral is a plane figure with four angles and four sides. The sum of the four interior angles of a quadrilateral is 360°. Two intersecting lines are called its diagonals.

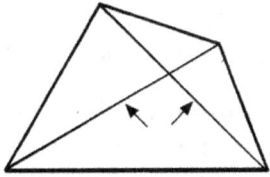

Q-28. What is the area of a triangle?
Ans. The area of a triangle is half the base multiplied by the corresponding altitude.

Quiz Time Mathematics

Q-29. What is the area of a rectangle and a square?
Ans. The area of the rectangle is equal to the length multiplied by height. Area of the square is equal to the side multiplied by side.

Q-30. What is a circle?
Ans. A circle is the path of a point which keeps a constant distance from a fixed point. This fixed point is called the centre and the path is called the circumference. The fixed distance is called the radius.

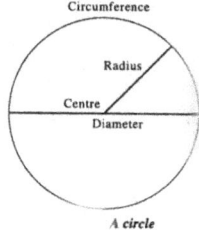

A circle

Q-31. What is the area of a circle?
Ans. The area of a circle is Πr^2 or $Pi(r)^2$ where 'r' is the radius of the circle.

Q-32. What is the area of a rhombus?
Ans. The area of a rhombus is half the product of the lengths of the two diagonals.

Q-33. What is a field book?
Ans. A book in which dimensions of fields are recorded to calculate areas is called a field book. For calculating the areas of fields, we usually come across triangles and trapeziums.

Q-34. What do you understand by the terms, radius, diameter, chord, secant, tangent and arc of a circle?
Ans.   (a) Radius : Distance between the centre and the circumference.
  (b) Diameter : The longest distance from one side of a circle to the other is called the diameter (Formula: $2\Pi r$). It is thus twice the radius.

Geometry

(c) Chord : A straight line joining any two points on the circumference.

(d) Secant : A straight line that cuts across the circumference or a circle at any two points.

(e) Tangent: A straight line that touches the circumference at one point only and has the same slope as the curve at the point of contact.

(f) Arc : A section of the circumference of a circle.

All these are shown in the figure below:

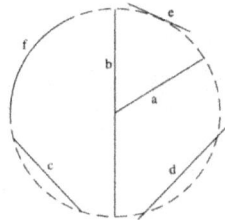

(a) Radius (b) Diameter (c) Chord (d) Secant (e) Tangent (f) Arc of a circle

Q-35. What is a semi-circle?

Ans. The space between a diameter and the circumference is called a semi-circle.

Q-36. How do we define a sector?

Ans. The space between any two radii is called a sector. Semi-circle, sector and segment are shown in the figure below:

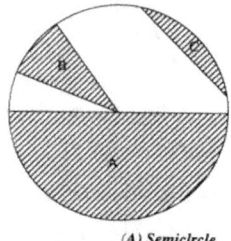

(A) Semicircle (B) Sector (C) Segment

Q-37. What is a segment?
Ans. The space between a chord and the circumference. (See the figure in the previous question.)

Q-38. When we put a dot with a lead pencil, is it not a geometric point?
Ans. No, it is not a geometric point, but a physical point. However, we make use of such points in geometry.

Q-39. What is a parabola?
Ans. The parabola is the path of a point, which moves so that its distance from a fixed line is always equal to its distance from a fixed point. In mathematics, a parabola is a curve formed by cutting a right circular cone with a plane parallel to the sloping side of the cone. The path of a bullet is a parabola.

Q-40. What is a hyperbola?
Ans. The hyperbola in geometry is a curve formed by cutting a right circular cone with a plane so that the angle between the plane and the base is greater than the angle between the base and the side of the cone. Ellipse, parabola and hyperbola are called conic sections, as shown in the figure below:

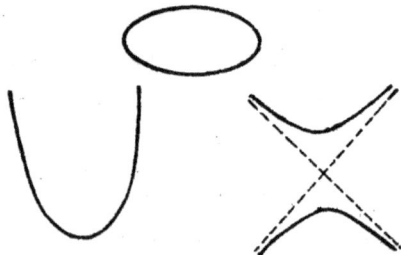

Q-41. What is a catenary?
Ans. The shape or curve taken by a chain or rope hanging freely between two points at the same height is known as a catenary. A suspension bridge makes a catenary.

Geometry

Q-42. How is an involute generated?
Ans. An involute is traced by the end of a piece of a sticky tape as it is unrolled of the spool.

Q-43. What is a cycloid?
Ans. A cycloid is the name given to the curve traced by a point on the outside edge of a wheel rolling along in a straight line.

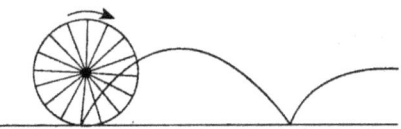

Q-44. What is a polygon?
Ans. A plane figure enclosed by several straight lines is called a polygon.

Q-45. What is a tetrahedron?
Ans. In geometry, it is a solid figure with four triangular faces; that is, a pyramid on a triangular base. A regular tetrahedron has equilateral triangles at its faces; it can be constructed by joining four points that are equidistant from each other on the surface of a sphere.

Q-46. What is a centroid?
Ans. The point of concurrence of medians in a triangle is called the centroid.

Q-47. What are the applications of geometry?
Ans. Geometry is used by designers, engineers, architects, surveyors and scientists.

Q-48. What is an orthocentre?
Ans. The point of concurrence of attitudes in a triangle is called an orthocentre.

Q-49. What is a circumcentre?
Ans. The point of concurrence of line bisectors in a triangle is called a circumcentre.

Q-50. What is incentre?
Ans. The point of concurrence of angle bisectors in a triangle is called an incentre.

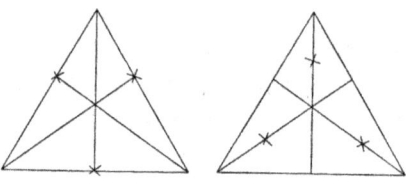

Geometry

Quizzes

1. The sum of the angles of a triangle is:
   - Ⓐ 180°
   - Ⓑ 200°
   - Ⓒ 360°
   - Ⓓ 2500
2. The sum of the angles of a hexagon is:
   - Ⓐ 420°
   - Ⓑ 360°
   - Ⓒ 720°
   - Ⓓ 270°
3. The sum of the external angle of an octagon is:
   - Ⓐ 360°
   - Ⓑ 180°
   - Ⓒ 720°
   - Ⓓ 270°
4. Who is called the Father of Geometry?
   - Ⓐ Pythagros
   - Ⓑ Euclid
   - Ⓒ Pappus
   - Ⓓ Euler
5. If the sum of two angles is 90°, they are.... angles.
   - Ⓐ Complementary
   - Ⓑ Supplementary
   - Ⓒ Adjacent
   - Ⓓ Alternate
6. Two angles, whose sum is 180° are called.......... angles.
   - Ⓐ Complementary
   - Ⓑ Supplementary
   - Ⓒ Adjacent
   - Ⓓ Alternate
7. Two lines cannot be said parallel if the pair of angles are equal.
   - Ⓐ Alternate
   - Ⓑ Corresponding

C Vertically opposite angles
D Sum of the interior angles of one side of the transversal line is 180 degrees.

8. A triangle whose two sides are equal is called............... triangle.
   A Equilateral   **B** Scalene
   C Isosceles   **D** Acute Angled

9. A triangle with all the three sides and angles equal, is called......triangle
   A Equilateral   **B** Scalene
   C Isosceles   **D** Right Angled

10. An angle with measure less than 90° is a/an……………..
    A Acute angle   **B** Obtuse angle
    C Right angle   **D** Complementary angle

11. An angle with measure more than 90° is a/an...............
    A Acute angle   **B** Obtuse angle
    C Right angle   **D** Complementary angle

12. An angle with measure more than 180°, but less than 360° is called a/an...............
    A Acute angle   **B** Obtuse angle
    C Straight angle   **D** Reflex angle

13. The .... angles are two angles whose sum is 360 degrees.
    A Conjugate angle   **B** Reflex angle
    C Acute angle   **D** Obtuse angle

14. The space between any two radii is called..........
    A Segment   **B** Sector
    C Chord   **D** Secant

Geometry

15. In the figure below, what does G represent?.

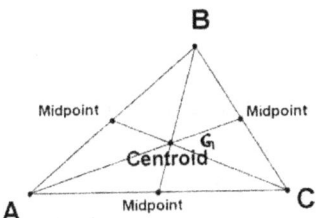

- Ⓐ Orthocentre
- Ⓑ Ampicentre
- Ⓒ Centroid
- Ⓓ Circumcentre

16. In the below figure, the point of intersection of altitude 0 is called - .

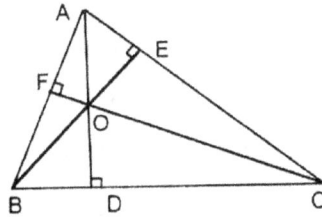

- Ⓐ Orthocentre
- Ⓑ Ambicentre
- Ⓒ Centroid
- Ⓓ Circumcentre

17. How many circles can be drawn through 3 non-collinear points.
- Ⓐ 1
- Ⓑ 2
- Ⓒ 3
- Ⓓ Many

18. Angle measure of a semi-circle is..........
- Ⓐ 45°
- Ⓑ 90°
- Ⓒ 180°
- Ⓓ 360°

19. The sum of either pair of opposite angles of a cyclic quadrilateral is:
- Ⓐ 90°
- Ⓑ 180°
- Ⓒ 270°
- Ⓓ 360°

Quiz Time Mathematics

20. The longest chord of a circle is a .... of the circle.
    - Ⓐ Tangent
    - Ⓑ Secant
    - Ⓒ Arc
    - Ⓓ Diameter

21. Which of the following formulae can be used to find the sum of the angles of n-gon.
    - Ⓐ S = 180 n - 360°
    - Ⓑ S = 360/n
    - Ⓒ S = 180+n
    - Ⓓ S = 540 + sn

22. The sum of all the exterior angle of a polygon is –
    - Ⓐ 180°
    - Ⓑ 360°
    - Ⓒ 540°
    - Ⓓ 720°

23. What is the name of the end of the proof box in a mathematical context?
    - Ⓐ QED
    - Ⓑ CPCT
    - Ⓒ WWW
    - Ⓓ RHS

24. In Lobachevsky-Bolyai Geometry, the sum of the angles of a triangle is..................
    - Ⓐ greater than 180°
    - Ⓑ less than 180°
    - Ⓒ equal to 180°
    - Ⓓ greater than 360°

25. In Riemannian non-Euclidean Geometry, the sum of the angles of a triangle is..........
    - Ⓐ greater than 180°
    - Ⓑ less than 180°
    - Ⓒ equal to 180°
    - Ⓓ greater than 360°

26. The line joining the midpoint of a side to its opposite vertex is called the ......
    - Ⓐ centroid
    - Ⓑ mean
    - Ⓒ median
    - Ⓓ orthocentre

27. Points lying on the same line are called:
    - Ⓐ intersecting points
    - Ⓑ collinear points
    - Ⓒ coincidents
    - Ⓓ contact points

Geometry

28.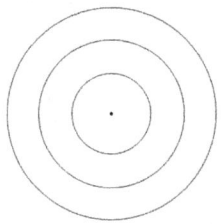

Circles having the same centre and different radii are called………..
- Ⓐ Collinear points
- Ⓑ Congruent points
- Ⓒ Tangent of a circle
- Ⓓ Concentric circles

29. **Points which lie on a common circle are:**
- Ⓐ Concyclic points
- Ⓑ Collinear points
- Ⓒ Concurrent points
- Ⓓ Tangents of circle

30. **If in two right triangles, the hypotenuse and one side of one triangle are equal to the hypotenuse and one side of the other triangle, then the two triangles are congruent. This congruence of triangles is called –**
- Ⓐ RHS Congruence Rule
- Ⓑ SAS Congruence Rule
- Ⓒ SSS Congruence Rule
- Ⓓ ASA Congruence Rule

31. **Identify the image.**

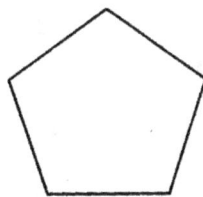

- Ⓐ Pentagon
- Ⓑ Regular pentagon
- Ⓒ Hexagon
- Ⓓ Octagon

Quiz Time Mathematics

32. What is the measure of each angle of Regular Octagon?
    - Ⓐ 120°
    - Ⓑ 150°
    - Ⓒ 140°
    - Ⓓ 135°

33. Which of the following is not the axiom of congruency of two triangles?
    - Ⓐ SSS
    - Ⓑ RHS
    - Ⓒ SA
    - Ⓓ LHS

34. What is the measure of each angle of an Equilateral Triangle?
    - Ⓐ 40°
    - Ⓑ 75°
    - Ⓒ 60°
    - Ⓓ 35°

35. How many squares can be drawn by using 9 dots:

    0 0 0

    0 0 0

    0 0 0

    - Ⓐ 3
    - Ⓑ 4
    - Ⓒ 9
    - Ⓓ 5

36. A figure having 14 faces with triangle and square is known as..............
    - Ⓐ dodecagon
    - Ⓑ cube
    - Ⓒ cuboctahedron
    - Ⓓ Icosidodecahedron

37. A figure having 32 faces with triangles and pentagons is called..............
    - Ⓐ dodecagon
    - Ⓑ cube
    - Ⓒ cuboctahedron
    - Ⓓ Icosidodecahetirnn

Geometry

38.

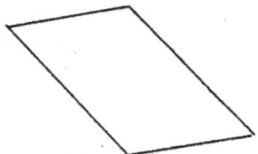

A quadrilateral with exactly two pairs of equal consecutive sides is called.............
- Ⓐ Rhombus
- Ⓑ Square
- Ⓒ Kite
- Ⓓ Rectangle

39. Which of the following is not true for a square?
- Ⓐ It is a rectangle with equal sides.
- Ⓑ The diagonals bisect at 90°.
- Ⓒ The diagonals are not equal.
- Ⓓ Its perimeter is 4 times the side.

40. What can you say about a quadrilateral with the following properties:
  a. All the sides are equal
  b. Diagonals are perpendicular to each other
  c. Diagonals bisect each other, but not equal
  This quadrilateral is a-0
- Ⓐ Square
- Ⓑ Rectangle
- Ⓒ Parallelogram
- Ⓓ Rhombus

41.

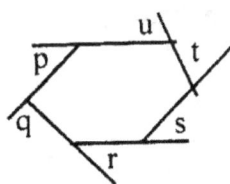

What is the sum of all the external angles: p + q + r + s + t + u?
- Ⓐ 180°
- Ⓑ 360°
- Ⓒ 425°
- Ⓓ 1375°

42. Two angles having a common side and common vertex and lying on opposite sides of their common side are called..............
    - Ⓐ Adjacent angles
    - Ⓑ Acute angles
    - Ⓒ Alternate angles
    - Ⓓ Linear pairs

43. Name the given figure.

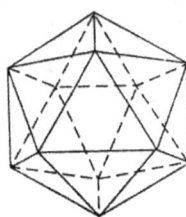

    - Ⓐ Polyhedron
    - Ⓑ Polynomial
    - Ⓒ Icosahedron
    - Ⓓ Octagon

44. Name the given polygon.

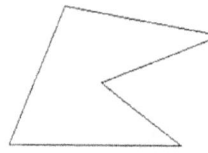

    - Ⓐ Pentagon
    - Ⓑ Concave
    - Ⓒ Convex
    - Ⓓ Quadrilateral

45. Name the above polygon.

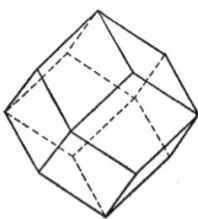

    - Ⓐ Icosahedrons
    - Ⓑ Polyhedron
    - Ⓒ Ditagon
    - Ⓓ Dodecahedron

Geometry

46. The point of concurrence of line bisectors in a triangle is called......

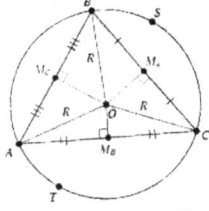

- Ⓐ Incentre
- Ⓑ Circumcentre
- Ⓒ Orthocentre
- Ⓓ Centroid

47. The point of concurrence of angle bisectors in a triangle is called...

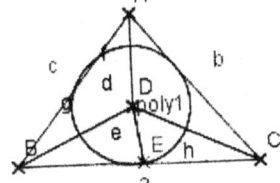

- Ⓐ Incentre
- Ⓑ Circumcentre
- Ⓒ Centroid
- Ⓓ Orthocentre

48. A theorem states:
In a right angle triangle, the square of hypotenuse is equal to the sum of squares of other two sides. Name the famous theorem?

- Ⓐ Thaler Therem
- Ⓑ Pythagoras Theorem
- Ⓒ Wallis Theorem
- Ⓓ Wilson Theorem

49. Name the angles?

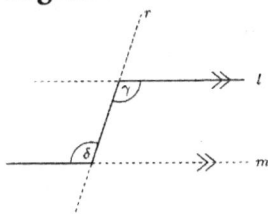

- Ⓐ Corresponding angles
- Ⓑ Alternate angles
- Ⓒ Polyhedral angles
- Ⓓ Complementary angles

50. A Pentagon is a.................. polygon.

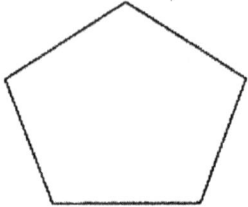

    Ⓐ Regular   Ⓑ Concave
    Ⓒ Convex   Ⓓ Irregular

51. The circle through the midpoints of the sides of a triangle, the feet of perpendiculars, from the vertices upon the sides, and the midpoints of the line segments between the vertices and the point of intersection is called...............

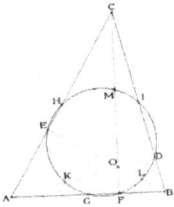

    Ⓐ Circum Circle   Ⓑ Incircle
    Ⓒ Concentric Circle   Ⓓ Nine-point circle

52. Name the only polygon in which the number of sides and diagonals are the same?

    Ⓐ Pentagon   Ⓑ Hexagon
    Ⓒ Octagon   Ⓓ Decagon

Geometry

Answers

1.	A	19.	B	37.	C
2.	C	20.	D	38.	C
3.	A	21.	A	39.	C
4.	B	22.	B	40.	D
5.	A	23.	A	41.	B
6.	B	24.	B	42.	A
7.	C	25.	A	43.	C
8.	C	26.	C	44.	B
9.	A	27.	B	45.	D
10.	A	28.	D	46.	B
11.	B	29.	A	47.	A
12.	D	30.	A	48.	B
13.	A	31.	B	49.	B
14.	B	32.	D	50.	C
15.	C	33.	D	51.	D
16.	A	34.	C	52.	D
17.	A	35.	D		
18.	B	36.	C		

ALGEBRA

$28\left(\frac{5x+78}{28}\right)$

$|2x-1| = |4x+3|$

$) = 28\left(\frac{5x+78}{28}\right)$

$2x-1 = +(4x+3) \underline{or} \; 2x-1 = -($

$) = 1(5x+78)$

$2x-1 = 4x+3$ $2x-1 = -$

$-20 = 5x-$

$-1 = 2x+3$ $6x-1 =$

$= 5x+78$

$-4 = 2x$ $6x =$

$-69 = $

$x = $ $y = $

$x = $

Algebra

Questions

Q-1. What is algebra?
Ans. The branch of mathematics dealing with the relationships and properties of number systems by the use of general symbols (such as: a, b, x, y) to represent mathematical quantities.

Q-2. How did the word algebra originate?
Ans. The word algebra originated in the 9th century A.D. from the title of the work on algebra by a Persian, Mohammed-ibn-Musa Al-Kwarizmi. He wrote a book in Arabic called *Kitab-Al-Jebr Wal muqabala*, which means *restoration* and *reduction*. In the course of time, the word *al-jebr* was changed to *algebra*. In its modem form, algebra was invented by the French mathematician, *Francois Viete* in the 16th century.

Q-3. Who was the first to work on the problems of equations?
Ans. A Greek mathematician, *Diophantus*, in the third century A.D. attempted some problems of equations. In fact, the basis of algebra were familiar in Babylon during 2000 B.C. and were practised by the Arabs in the middle ages.

Q-4. Who used the vowels and the consonants for the first time in algebra?
Ans. Francois Vieta, a French mathematician of the 16th century used the vowels *a,e,i,o,u* and the consonants *b,c,d,f,g* to represent unknown numbers.

Q-5. What are the three fundamental laws in algebra, which govern the addition, subtraction, multiplication and division of all numbers?
Ans. The three fundamental laws are: (a). Commutative laws of addition and multiplication, (b). Associative laws of addition and multiplication, (c). Distributive laws of multiplication.

Q-6. Who proposed the system of algebraic symbols?
Ans. The great 17th century French philosopher, *Rene Descartes* proposed the system of algebraic symbols now in use.

Q-7. What is the system proposed by Descartes?
Ans. In his system, a, b, c, etc., represent the fixed numbers and x,y,z stand for the unknown numbers in a problem.

Q-8. What are the commutative laws of addition and multiplication?
Ans. According to the commutative law of addition, a+b= b+a and according to the commutative law of multiplication a×b= b×a.

Q-9. What are the associative laws of addition and multiplication?
Ans. According to the associative laws of addition and multiplication, a+(b+c)= (a+b)+c and a×(b×c)=(a×b)×c.

Q-10. What is the distributive law of multiplication?
Ans. According to the distributive law of multiplication, a×(b+c)=a×b+a×c.

Q-11. Can we find out HCF and LCM of algebraic expressions?
Ans. Yes, HCF and LCM are found out by following the methods of arithmetic.

Q-12. What is the meaning of a^2 and a^3?
Ans. The meaning of a^2 is that 'a' is being multiplied with 'a' two times, i.e, a^2=a×a. a^3 means that 'a' is being multiplied with 'a' three times, i.e., a^3=a×a×a.

Algebra

Q-13. What is the value of any number raised to the power zero?
Ans. Any number raised to the power zero is equal to one, e.g. $a^0 = 1$.

Q-14. What is the value of a^{m+n}?
Ans. $a^{m+n} = a^m \times a^n$

Q-15. What is the meaning of $(a^m)^n$?
Ans. $(a^m)^n$ is equal to a^{mn}, e.g., $(a^2)^3 = a^6$.

Q-16. What is the value of a^{-m}?
Ans. $a^{-m} = \dfrac{1}{a^m}$

Q-17. What is the value of $(ab)^m$?
Ans. $(ab)^m = a^m b^m$

Q-18. What is the value of a^m/a^n?
Ans. $\dfrac{a^m}{a^n} = a^m \times a^{-n} = a^{m-n}$

Q-19. When + is multiplied by +, what is the result?
Ans. When + is multiplied by + the result is '+'.

Q-20. When – is multiplied by –, what is the result?
Ans. When – is multiplied by – the result is '+'.

Q-21. When + is multiplied by –, what is the result?
Ans. When + is multiplied by –, the result is '–'.

Q-22. What are complex numbers?
Ans. The numbers which contain real part and imaginary part are called complex numbers.

Q-23. What is a conjugate complex number?
Ans. If $a+ib$ is a complex number then $a - ib$ is called its conjugate complex. We obtain conjugate complex by changing the sign of the imaginary part.

Q-24. When are the two complex numbers said to be equal?
Ans. When the real and the imaginary parts of a complex number are equal to the real and the imaginary parts of the other complex number, they are said to be equal.

Q-25. Who devised the method of algebraic reasoning during the 19th century?
Ans. The British mathematician, George Boole used the method first, in working out construction of computers.

Q-26. What is Inverse Operation?
Ans. If two operations negate each other, they are termed as inverse operation. Addition and subtraction are inverse operations.

Q-27. What is an additive inverse of 4 complex number?
Ans. It is that complex number which when added to a given complex number, the result is zero.

Q-28. What is multiplicative inverse?
Ans. It is a complex number which when multiplied with the given complex number, the result is zero.

Q-29. What are the cube roots of unity?
Ans. 1, w, w2 are the cube roots of unity, where,

$$w = \frac{-1+\sqrt{-3}}{2} \text{ and } w^2 = \frac{-1-\sqrt{-3}}{2}$$

The sum of I+w+w² = 0 and their product is equal to one.

Q-30. What is an equation?
Ans. An equation may be looked upon as a balance with equal numerical values on each side of the 'equal' sign (=).

Algebra

Q-31. How many equations are required to solve 'n' unknowns?
Ans. We need 'n' equations to solve 'n' unknowns. In other words, the number of equations should be equal to the number of unknowns.

Q-32. What are the cubic equations?
Ans. The cubic equations are those in a single variable which appears to the power 3, but not higher.

Q-33. What is the degree of an equation?
Ans. Generally, the degree of an equation is defined as the sum of the exponents of the variables in the highest power term of the equation.

Q-34. How are operations carried out on equations?
Ans. All operations of addition, subtraction, multiplication or division are carried out on all members of an equation, meaning that we should add or subtract or multiply or divide the whole equation by the same quantity.

Q-35. What is a linear equation?
Ans. The linear equation is that in which no variable term is raised to a power higher than 1 (one).

Q-36. What is a quadratic equation?
Ans. If the highest power of the unknown quantity is two, it is called a quadratic equation. A quadratic equation always has two roots.

Q-37. What is an algebraic identity?
Ans. When an equation is true for all the replacement values of the variables concerned, it is called an identity.

Q-38. Which is the most familiar identity?
Ans. The most familiar identity is $(a+b)^2 = a^2 + 2ab + b^2$.

Q-39. What is the value of $(a-b)^2$
Ans. $(a-b)^2 = a^2 - 2ab + b^2$.

Q-40. What are the factors of $a^2 - b^2$?
Ans. $a^2 - b^2 = (a+b)(a-b)$

Q-41. What is the value of $(a+b)^3$?
Ans. $(a+b)^3 = a^3 + 3a^2b + 3ab^2 + b^3$.

Q-42. What is the value of $(a-b)^3$?
Ans. $(a-b)^3 = a^3 - 3a^2b + 3ab^2 - b^3$.

Q-43. What are the factors of $a^3 - b^3$?
Ans. $a^3 - b^3 = (a-b)(a^2 + b^2 + ab)$.

Q-44. What are the factors of $a^3 + b^3$?
Ans. $a^3 + b^3 = (a+b)(a^2 - ab + b^2)$.

Q-45. What is harmonic series?
It is an inverse of arithmetic series.

Q-46. What are sequences and series?
Ans. A sequence is a succession of numbers and a series is a sum of numbers in a sequence.

Q-47. What is an arithmetic series?
Ans. In a series, if the difference of any two consecutive terms is the same, it is called an arithmetic series, e.g. 2, 4, 6, 8, 10, ... Most series are "infinite" — containing an infinite number of terms.

Q-48. Imagine a cement foundation that is 16cm above the level of the ground. On this foundation, you build up 6 layers of stone blocks. Each layer is 8cm thick. As you add each layer of blocks, the height of the pile becomes larger. What would be the form of equation if x represents the number of layers and y represents the height of the pile?
Ans. It will be a linear equation $y = 8x + 16$. (See Figure)

Algebra

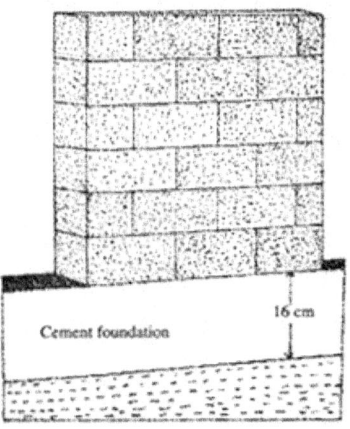

Q-49. What is a geometric series?
Ans. In a series, if the ratio of any two consecutive terms is constant, it is called a geometrical series, e.g. 2, 4, 8, 16, 32,

Q-50. What are the uses of algebra?
Ans. Algebra has proved very useful in solving the problems of physics, chemistry, engineering, finance, probability, equations, etc.

Q-51. How would you solve the two equations, 2y=x+4 and y=5 - x graphically?
Ans. Take the equation, 2y=x+4 and give the different values to x and correspondingly find the values of y:

x	0	2	4
y	2	3	4

Do the same for the equation y=5 - x

x	0	3	5
y	5	2	0

Quiz Time Mathematics

Draw the graph (Fig.). The point of intersection represents the values of x and y.

Value of x= 2

and y =3

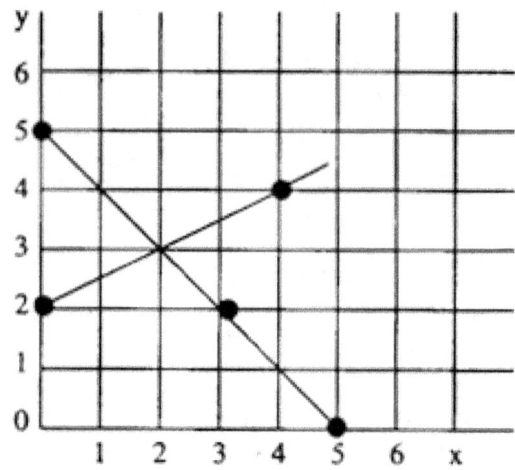

Algebra

Quizzes

1. Which among the following theorem is also known as BPT (Basic Proportionality Theorem)?
   - **A** Pythagoras Theorem
   - **B** Wilson Theorem
   - **C** Congruence Theorem
   - **D** Thales Theorem

2. Which of the following is the Cartesian Equation of asteroid curve?
   - **A** $x^{2/3} + y^{2/3} = a^{2/3}$
   - **B** $r = a^2 \theta$
   - **C** $x^2 + y^2 = r^2$
   - **D** $\dfrac{x^2}{a^2} + \dfrac{y^2}{b^2} = 1$

3. Which of the following represent a circle?
   - **A** $\dfrac{x^2}{a^2} + \dfrac{y^2}{b^2} = 1$
   - **B** $\dfrac{x^2}{a^2} - \dfrac{y^2}{b^2} = 1$
   - **C** $(x-b)^2 + (y-k)^2 = r^2$
   - **D** $x^{2/3} + y^{2/3} = 1$

4. Which of the following represent the equation of a Catenary?
   - **A** $y = x^2 + r^2$
   - **B** $r = 2a(1+\cos\theta)$
   - **C** $y = a\cos h \dfrac{x}{a}$
   - **D** $x = a\,\cos^2 t$

Quiz Time Mathematics

5. The Parametric Equation of circle is:
   - (A) $x = a\cos^3 t, y = a\sin^3 t$
   - (B) $x = t-1, y = t^2+1$
   - (C) $x = \sin\theta, y = a\cos\theta$
   - (D) $x = o \ s^3\theta$

6. Every integer greater than 2 can be represented as the sum of two primes:
   Who stated the above conjecture?
   - (A) Euler
   - (B) Goldbach
   - (C) Banach
   - (D) De Moivre

7. What is the Cartesian Equation of the curve Kampyle of Eudoxus?
   - (A) $y^2 + x^2 = r^2$
   - (B) $a^2 b^2 = X^2 b^2 + Y^2 a^2$
   - (C) $a^2 x^4 = b^4(X^2 + y^2)$
   - (D) $y^2(a+x) = x^2(3a-x)$

8. "Every integer is equal to the sum of not more than 9 cubes. Also every integer is the sum of not more than 19 fourth powers and so on....." Who stated this theorem?
   - (A) Wilson
   - (B) Waring
   - (C) Goldwich
   - (D) Fermat

9. If p is prime then $1+(p-1)!$ is divisible by p, whose statement is this?
   - (A) Waring
   - (B) Goldbich
   - (C) Fermat
   - (D) Wilson

10. The Fundamental Theorem of Algebra that "Every m degree polynomial has m roots" was proved by-
    - (A) Euler
    - (B) Gauss
    - (C) Galois
    - (D) Gunter

11. Which theorem in mathematics had the other names such as: "Bride's chair" or "Figure of Bride"?
    - (A) Thaler Theorem
    - (B) Pythagoras Theorem
    - (C) Congruence Theorem
    - (D) Wilson Theorem

Algebra

12. To whom is the first theorem relating to circles attributed?
    - Ⓐ Thales
    - Ⓑ Pythagoras
    - Ⓒ Apollonius
    - Ⓓ Agnesi

13. Which law is followed by the bee in building the wax cells of honey comb?
    - Ⓐ Maxima and Minima
    - Ⓑ Gravitational law
    - Ⓒ Algebraic law
    - Ⓓ Law of large numbers

14. There is a famous theorem $(\cos x + i \sin x)^n = \cos nx + i \sin nx$ in trigonometry bearing the name of one of the famous French mathematician. What was his name?
    - Ⓐ Abraham De Moivre
    - Ⓑ Nicholus Chuquet
    - Ⓒ Michel Chasles
    - Ⓓ Shanks

15. The series, $\theta = \tan\theta + \frac{1}{3}\tan^3\theta + \frac{1}{5}\tan^5\theta$ bears the name of a mathematician. What was his name?
    - Ⓐ Newton
    - Ⓑ Gregory
    - Ⓒ Kelvin
    - Ⓓ Galileo

16. The best known paradox of Achilles and the Tortoise is also known as:
    - Ⓐ Rubike Paradox
    - Ⓑ Zeno Paradox
    - Ⓒ Fuclid Paradox
    - Ⓓ Diophantus Curve

17. Which theorem is also known as 'Laws of Large Numbers'?
    - Ⓐ Poisson
    - Ⓑ Bernoulli
    - Ⓒ Cauchy
    - Ⓓ Pythagoras

18. What is the curve $r^2 = a^2\theta$ known?
    - Ⓐ Limacon
    - Ⓑ Fen-nat's spiral
    - Ⓒ Cardiod
    - Ⓓ Foliumd

19. Which of the following is the equation of Newton's diverging Parabolas?
    - (A) $y = 4ax$
    - (B) $ay^2 = x(x^2 - 2bx + C)$
    - (C) $x^2 = 4ay$
    - (D) $r = a(1 + \cos?)$

20. The graph of the equation r=a sin2 or r˭a cos2 is:
    - (A) a four leafed rose
    - (B) a three folded rose
    - (C) an eight folded rose
    - (D) a two leafed rose

21. $X^n + Y^n = Z^n$, where n>2 has no solution and x ,y ,z are integers. The famous equation is known as –
    - (A) Fermat's last theorem
    - (B) Fennat's first theorem
    - (C) Pappu's theorem
    - (D) Piano's theorem

22. Which of the following is the equation of the circle?
    - (A) $X^2 = 4ay$
    - (B) $ax^2 + bx + c = 0$
    - (C) $x^2 + y^2 = a^2$
    - (D) $ax + by + c = 0$

23. The polar equation of the Leminiscate of Bernoulli is:
    - (A) $ax + by + c = 0$
    - (B) $r = a \sin 2\theta$
    - (C) $r^2 = a^2 \cos 2\theta$
    - (D) $r = a(1 + \cos \theta)$

24. What is the name of the curve whose equation is $X^{2/3} + Y^{2/3} = a^{2/3}$?
    - (A) Circle
    - (B) Cycloid
    - (C) Limacon
    - (D) Hypocycloid

25. What is the polar equation of the Parabolic Spiral discovered by Fermat?
    - (A) $r = a(1 + \cos \theta)$
    - (B) $r = a \sin 2\theta$
    - (C) $r^2 = a^2 \theta$
    - (D) $r^2 = \theta$

Algebra

26. If a hexagon is inscribed in a conic, the three points of intersection of pairs of opposite sides lie on a line-what is the name of this famous theorem?
    - Ⓐ Fermat Theorem
    - Ⓑ Pascal Theorem
    - Ⓒ Simpson Theorem
    - Ⓓ Newtonian Theorem

27. Which one of the following is the example of an open curve?
    - Ⓐ Circle
    - Ⓑ Ellipse
    - Ⓒ Parabola
    - Ⓓ Cardioid

Quiz Time Mathematics

Answers

1.	D	10.	B	19.	B
2.	A	11.	B	20.	A
3.	C	12.	A	21.	A
4.	C	13.	A	22.	C
5.	C	14.	A	23.	C
6.	B	15.	B	24.	D
7.	C	16.	B	25.	C
8.	B	17.	B	26.	B
9.	D	18.	B	27.	D

  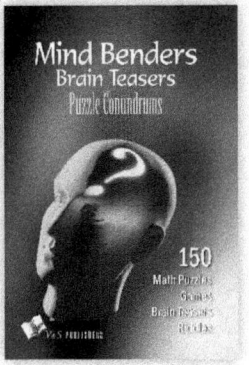

Author: Manasvi Vohra
Format: Paperback
Language: English
Pages: 184
Price: ₹ 110.00

Author: Manasvi Vohra
Format: Paperback
Language: English
Pages: 144
Price: ₹ 110.00

Author: Vikas Khatri
Format: Paperback
Language: English
Pages: 152
Price: ₹ 110.00

History is something that occurred in the past which is memorable, or remarkable, good or bad. The word, history is basically used for a record of events that happened in the past.

In the book, Quiz Time History, there are about 1100 interesting, knowledge-based questions with answers that will educate the readers about the significant historical facts and incidents that took place during the Early Indian Historical Period, The Medieval Times and the Modern Era.

India, as we all know is a vast country with a rich culture, heritage and historical background.

The study of environment is important for us as we are an integral part of the environment. It includes composite physical and biological sciences including subjects, such as Ecology, Botany, Zoology, Physics, Chemistry, Soil Science, Geography, etc. Environmental studies also incorporate human relationships, perceptions and policies towards the environment. Hence, in order to understand and learn more about the environment; and to find answers queries people consider mysteries nature, Environment Quiz Book is an ideal one.

The book includes several interesting and simple:
- Questions & Answers
- MCQs • Fill in the Blanks
- Crossword • Word Search
- True & False

- Enjoy mental workouts?
- Like numerical brain teasers?
- Dabble in solving puzzles?
- Use maths occasionally?
- Accept intellectual challenges?
- Love solving riddles?

It "YES" to any of these questions, then this is the right book for you! Also if you want to test your logical skills and also to have fun, then read this collection of brain teasers and check out how smart you are!!

---

visit our online bookstore: www.vspublishers.com

Author: Rajeev Garg & Amit Garg
Format: Paperback
Language: English
Pages: 192
Price: ₹ 96.00

That is what your child will find in this Science Quiz Book — brilliant ideas brimming with the latest information and simple explanations of fascinating facts and feats about our constantly evolving world.

Designed to boost your child's knowledge base, each page comes alive with new facts in an engrossing form of short Questions and Answers with explanatory illustrations, all of which makes it easy to read, easy to follow and easy to remember.

Author: Ivar Utial
Format: Paperback
Language: English
Pages: 127
Price: ₹ 120.00

Enliven your leisure hours with QuizTime! It guarantees you to give many hours of exciting mind storming quiz games. Excel your ability to hold social meetings with charisma and quiz gaming. This book employs tested quiz skills in very well-defined structure for easy comprehension. The book is aimed to cater to a large section of the society.

Author: Gladys Ambat
Format: Paperback
Language: English
Pages: 256
Price: ₹ 120.00

Quiz and puzzles are brain fitness fundas of a unique kind! The thrill to win or lose gaming session of a quiz programme can give you an optimum level of mental fitness and alertness. You simply bubble over with the sheer joy of challenge.

The book is a lively presentation for all youngsters and a pleasant leisure companion for the elders. The veteran author has put together over 4000 exciting quizzes and interesting brain-teasers to get you all keyed up. While you race through every page — you could find yourself sitting on the edge of the chair. Yet, you get charged with a spirit of challenge to unearth hidden answers or solve uncharted problems by your latent thinking power.

visit our online bookstore: www.vspublishers.com

Author: Saurabh Aggrwal
Format: Paperback
Language: English
Pages: 256
Price: ₹ 200.00

Author: Dr. Nivedita Ganguli
Format: Paperback
Language: English
Pages: 108
Price: ₹ 96.00

Author: V. Rajesh
Format: Paperback
Language: English
Pages: 104
Price: ₹ 120.00

Did you know that crossword puzzles first appeared in the New York World in 1913, and soon became a popular feature in newspapers? Did you know that Kellog's as a brand had spent $90,000 on advertising, more than 100 years ago in 1906, including one $4000 a page ad in the Ladies Home Journal. Apple had lured John Sculley away from Pepsi because they wanted him to apply his marketing skills to the personal computer market and not on fizz drinks. Find facts and trivia from the world of business that will amaze and delight you. The questions in this book have been framed in a way that they are: guessable with intelligent, lateral thinking; interesting, amusing, and surprising.

Do you feel that life sometimes pulls you down? Do you keep on searching for some light to pull you out of darkness? Do you feel so wrapped up in your own issues that you miss out the real treasures of life? Probably this book may create a full-stop to your search. The episodes present in the book would enable you to see life from a brighter perspective. The 'In a Nutshell' portion following each episode would give direction towards Life Management. Quotations present in form of 'Food for Thought' would give rich nutrition to your thought process. Our wrong perspective towards everyday issues makes life more complicated. Changing perspective would enable us to live life fully.

It is easy to skip a question during an exam if it is "Out of Syllabus" but what do you do when faced with a situation in life for which you were not given any input? Can you run away from the situation hiding behind the "Out of Syllabus" excuse?

Career is one area where one is expected to know and manage contingencies. After all a person is paid to handle things and deliver results. The reality is that most people get a lot of academic and conceptual inputs relating to one's career choice but very little practical inputs on how to effectively use the academic learning.

visit our online bookstore: www.vspublishers.com

Also available in Hindi, Bangla, Tamil	Also available in Hindi	Also available in Hindi
Author: Dr. C.L. Garg/ Amit Garg Format: Paperback Language: English Pages: 120 Price: ₹ 140.00	Author: Vikas Khatri Format: Paperback Language: English Pages: 160 Price: ₹ 150.00	Author: Ivar Utial Format: Paperback Language: English Pages: 120 Price: ₹ 96.00

Science projects and models play a pivotal role in inculcating scientific temper in young minds and in harnessing their skills. school students of senior classes have to work on such projects and these carry much weight in their overall performance.

All these aspects have been considered during the compilation of the projects and models. This book will also be an ideal choice for parents interested in enhancing scientific temper of their children; and for hobbyists.

The book has 81 Classroom projects on: Physics, Chemistry, Biology & Electronics for Sec. & Sr. Sec. Students

A study of Science and Scientific theories is almost incomplete without relevant and methodical Experiments. In fact, experiments are an inseparable part of any scientific study or research. In this book, the author has tried to simplify science to the readers, particularly the school-going students, through easy and interesting experiments. The experiments given in the book are based on one scientific phenomena or another, such as atmospheric pressure, high and low temperatures, boiling, freezing and melting points of solids, liquids, gases, gravitational force, magnetism, electricity, solubility of substances, etc.

Supplementary science books not only interest and excite young students, but also stimulate their interest in the subject.

This exciting book shows you how to have fun with 101 Science Games. There is little doubt that science experiments can be quite interesting and useful in discovering mysteries of nature.

The book is fully illustrated with step-by-step instructions to give you first hand experience of making simple scientific equipments like :

Telescope
Barometer
Hectometer
Model Electric Motor
Electroscope
Periscope
Steam Turbine; and more...

visit our online bookstore: www.vspublishers.com

Also available in Hindi

Author: Vikas Khatri Format: Paperback Language: English Pages: 120 Price: ₹ 100.00	Author: Prosenjit Saha Format: Paperback Language: English Pages: 108 Price: ₹ 295.00	Author: A.H. Hashmi Format: Paperback Language: English Pages: 122 Price: ₹ 150.00

54 cool and Challenging art working, projects, crafts, experiments and more for kids!!!

Unplugging kids from their MP3 players and game systems for one-on-one family time is a great way to reconnect in today's hectic world. And what better way to spend time together than doing an activity that's not only fun but also promotes creativity and self-expression?

Greatest Crafts and Projects for Children is packed with 54 craft projects ranging from outdoor projects to gifts and party favours to holiday decor to projects that promote learning through play with step-by-step instructions to guide children to successful completion of each project.

We believe everyone can draw or paint. Of course some people are naturally talented but we are all capable of channelling our artistic skills and creativity.

With this belief in mind, we have published this Drawing and Painting Course Volume II for children who want to learn and master the art in a fun way. This book starts with the basics – lines, shades, texture, balance, harmony, rhythm, tone, colours, etc., and goes on to teach the various different techniques of drawing and painting with step-by-step instructions, accompanied by an audio-visual CD.

Children have always been attracted towards bright colours, various shapes and diverse objects that they see around them. Nature fascinates them. The beautiful birds, animals, flowers and trees fire their imagination and they want to capture it on paper. But how, for all are not artists by birth.

Well, this book has been especially developed for those who want to learn and master the art in a fun way. The step-by-step instructions, along with the audio-visual CD, will show you how to create beautiful pictures. See how a circle or an oval transforms into a flower or a peacock; a few lines here, and a few there become a human figure.

visit our online bookstore: www.vspublishers.com

www.ingramcontent.com/pod-product-compliance
Lightning Source LLC
Chambersburg PA
CBHW070337230426
43663CB00011B/2357